Moving
Beyond

Moving Beyond

ACCESS YOUR INTUITION, PSYCHIC
ABILITY AND SPIRIT CONNECTION

Fleur Leussink

First published in Great Britain in 2021 by Yellow Kite
An Imprint of Hodder & Stoughton
An Hachette UK company

1

A CIP catalogue record for this title is available from the British Library

Hardback ISBN 978 1 529 36695 2
eBook ISBN 978 1 529 36696 9

Typeset in Sabon MT by Hewer Text UK Ltd, Edinburgh
Printed and bound in Great Britain by Clays Ltd, Elcograf S.p.A.

Hodder & Stoughton policy is to use papers that are natural, renewable and recyclable products and made from wood grown in sustainable forests. The logging and manufacturing processes are expected to conform to the environmental regulations of the country of origin.

Yellow Kite
Hodder & Stoughton Ltd
Carmelite House
50 Victoria Embankment
London EC4Y 0DZ

www.yellowkitebooks.co.uk

Frits

Marietje

Harry

Tony

Piet

Elise

Pat

Alex

Phoebe

In every class, you are the true teachers

CONTENTS

Introduction

To mention at a party that I communicate with people who have passed over is a conversation-stopping career confession. Once people have recovered, I'm always told that my job is wildly unexpected because I look and seem surprisingly 'normal.' They are also surprised to discover that I was a sceptic. Perhaps even more contradictory is that I have been working as a psychic medium for ten years and have done readings for over 15,000 people, and yet I still have a layer of scepticism I can't shake. If you're someone who's sceptical of psychic readings and communicating with spirits, believe me, so am I. While I've given psychic mediumship readings to people from all walks of life, from mothers' bereavement groups to A-list celebrities, I still wonder: *Is it real?*

EARLY LIFE

I was not a sceptic as a child. Kids aren't sceptical by nature. They are still connected to the spirit within. I was no different, except that my world was probably not your world. I saw colours around living people, and I saw the deceased. It wasn't too hard to hide my secret from the outside world because in all other ways, I was an ordinary six-year-old. I had bangs framing chubby cheeks, was often precocious, and had a deep dislike of napping.

I spent the first seven years of my childhood in the Netherlands and then moved to Houston, Texas. These were sweet years and my parents took my spirit encounters in their stride. At home, I was free to share what I saw and felt, but I quickly learned to keep my experiences to myself at school. Thankfully, my parents never made me feel like I was wrong or strange. My mum had always been interested in the metaphysical and tackled the problem by buying a lot of New Age books to help her understand. Convinced by what his mediumistic child was saying, my dad frequently took me to the store to pick lottery numbers. We never won the lottery (my mum told him with exasperation that wasn't the point of my gift), but we had a lot of fun trying. I know that I would not be the psychic medium I am today without their support.

As I got older, the spirit visitations became less and less frequent. I turned my focus to becoming a doctor instead. Winning a Coca-Cola Scholars Foundation scholarship allowed me to enter UCLA as a premedical student and neuroscience major. I was relieved; I had not seen, felt or heard anything out of the ordinary in many years, long enough to convince myself I'd imagined it.

Things were going well until I unexpectedly became very sick in my first year of college. My symptoms had appeared out of nowhere and no doctor could figure out what was going on. In an act of pure desperation, I made an appointment with a psychic medium. Without knowing a thing about me, she said, 'You are a psychic medium. You're not living your purpose and if you don't, your body will become very ill and you can possibly die.' I was taken aback. Not because she was telling me I was a psychic medium, I knew that. I was taken aback because the prospect of dying was not something I relished. I walked out of her office so angry that a power greater than me seemed to be ruling my life. But, I didn't want to die, so I started meditating. Ironically, it was this fear of death that jump-started my efforts to understand my gift and ultimately led to my career of communicating with the dead.

MY FIRST READINGS

I did not find it easy to accept that I was a psychic medium. I was confused, scared and angry. I was also incredibly sceptical and this disbelief increased when I learned in my college classes how easy it is for our brains to believe things that aren't there. I decided to run an experiment on myself. I decided to start offering readings for free, to look at the psychic and spirit information rationally, analyse the reality of each situation, and hope to answer the question: *Is it real?*

My first ever readings were done from a tiny walk-in closet in a shared college room. While my room-mate completed her Spanish homework, I did readings over the phone in the closet with my clothes pressed into my back. In those initial years, I lived in terror that somehow my friends would find out. I hesitated to tell my room-mates what I was really doing in the closet for hours at a time, but I decided that disappearing into a tiny closet for hours for no reason was somehow less strange. Luckily, they were surprisingly excited when they learned the truth.

I couldn't see my clients' faces; sessions were done over the phone, and all they were allowed to relay back to me was 'yes' or 'no'. After a reading, I would put on my 'scientist hat' and listen back to the recording I made for each encounter. I wrote down each fact I mentioned in the reading, and each was given a score. Doing the maths, I measured my percentage of accuracy over the duration of the reading. I'll spare you the nerdy standard deviations and just tell you I was surprised to find that I was tallying up at 80–95 per cent accuracy. I was intrigued. For the first time, I allowed myself to think that maybe there was something to this whole spirit thing.

The thing I could not measure was the impact. People wrote thank-you cards saying their life was changed, they'd stopped using antidepressants, or they felt like they were alive for the first time in years. I cried when I received a card from a man who hadn't even had a reading. 'Thank you for giving me my wife back,' he wrote, 'she's been lost to us since the death of our son ten years ago. My other children have their mother back.' These words of gratitude made such an impact on my spirit and I realised that while this drastic job change was nothing I thought I wanted, it was everything my spirit craved.

In all the time that I had spent worried about the realness of a spirit world, I had never fully considered the need for healing through this work. What was even more striking was that I never

4

felt like I was creating the connection between my client and their loved ones, it had always existed. I was the translator; my job was to act as a bridge and facilitate a reunion between my client and their loved one in spirit or to their own spirit. No one was ever disconnected, they had only forgotten their way back home.

CLOSURE AND HEALING

At a party, someone once told me, 'It's not that I don't believe, I just don't see the point.' I was struck by this perspective because it is the opposite of how I feel. I absolutely continue to have days of scepticism, but I never waver on why I'm doing this work. I work for the closure and I continue on because it changes people's lives.

It's emotional when I connect someone to their loved ones in spirit. It isn't a party trick or a mentalist magic show; it feels sacred. I have witnessed healing, growth and relief. This closure is a real thing, and health professionals have seen the difference it can make. To my initial surprise, clients have frequently told me they have been referred to me by a therapist or doctor. In return, I often recommend mental health professionals and resources to my clients.

I feel so honoured that people choose to sit in front of me with their deepest vulnerabilities exposed. Almost every single person cries. I vividly remember Tony, a 250-pound muscle man with tattoos covering his face, bawling his eyes out in my office when I told him his mother was there in spirit. I wasn't expecting this tough guy to cry, but he was overcome with emotion when his mum told him it was okay that he missed her final moments while he was in prison. Tony's mum assured him she loved him. People leave their sessions, like Tony, with puffy eyes and tear-stained cheeks so often that a few weeks after I started working in an office, the receptionist (not knowing what I did) asked me what I was doing to them.

It is hard to describe what happens within the four walls of my little office. To start, there is no sage, the room is well lit, and it looks like a regular therapist's office. In my office, all are welcome. Many different kinds of people have sat on my couch, tough guys like Tony as well as A-list celebrities. I've come to realise that no matter what you look like or how high your celebrity status is, we have all loved and lost, and we are all looking for meaning in our own lives.

I have personally been amazed and baffled by some of the consequences of a reading, because they can have far-reaching domino effects. Perhaps the clearest example of the effects a reading can have is that of Grace, a woman in her fifties who had always known she was adopted. Grace had spent her early twenties hiring private investigators because neither of her parents had been listed on her birth certificate. Grace signed up for 23andMe and Ancestry in the years that followed but she consistently met dead ends in trying to find her father.

Many years later, Grace heard about me through a friend and signed up for a reading. In recounting the story to me she said, 'you were quiet, and after some time you said, "I don't see your biological father as being passed. I don't think he is in the spirit world. I think he is alive. In fact, he's not in the same state that you live in and I am getting the name Robert." You said it so matter-of-factly that there was no other response other than to look one last time.' Grace hired a private investigator later that day. She typed in Robert on the form, the name she had received in the reading, and her own birthdate. The very next day she received a call: 'We found your father, his name is Robert, and he lives in West Virginia.' Grace and her biological father now speak every day; they have reunited other members of their family and he calls her his miracle.

I too think it is a miracle. I don't get bored of these stories; they seem incredible even to me and I lived them.

TEACHING OTHERS

I have put the question, *Is it real?* on ice, in favour of the question, *How does it work?*

I realised that the question, *Is psychic mediumship real?* is rather futile and limiting. It is futile because it is impossible to prove that anything outside of our physical reality exists; we are bound to it. We cannot remove ourselves and study our existence from a body-less angle. It is limiting because we cannot explore how extrasensory perception works if we don't believe it exists.

Anecdotally, *Is it real?* is answered with an easy and clear YES. I have my own experiences, but I know that everyone else does too. At a party, when I have admitted to working as a psychic medium, nearly every person will respond by telling me about *some* experience in which they felt, saw or heard the unexplainable. Even the most disbelieving person has one or two stories of a moment that seems illogical, inexplicable or maybe a little magical. Each of these stories are told to me with a disclaimer, such as, 'don't think I am weird, but . . .', 'I am a really logical person, yet . . .', or 'I have never told anyone this . . .' I understand, they don't want to be seen as crazy.

It doesn't surprise me that nearly everyone has at least one experience; I know that the ability to sense something beyond the five senses is an innate ability everyone has and can expand upon. I have taught thousands of people and offered them tools to connect to their intuitive and psychic skills and to feel their loved ones in spirit more clearly. Anyone can learn, there are no exceptions. That doesn't mean I am training everyone to work as a psychic medium – the vast majority of my students are not taking my classes to do readings for other people. My students want to understand the fleeting intuitive moments they already have. They wish to come home to themselves and find the answers within themselves, rather than look for answers in the external world. They crave a more consistent connection to their loved ones in spirit.

Not everyone who develops these skills needs to work as a psychic medium; that would be like saying every person who enjoys exercise needs to go run a marathon. Yet, the joy of moving your body is a joy I wish everyone to experience. In the same way, I wish for everyone to feel what it is to connect to your inner voice and your loved ones on the other side. This is not a weird gift, it is your natural way of being.

Finding your way back to your spirit and to the spirit world at large can feel like coming home. I have witnessed it turn students' lives around. When I work with someone who is not in alignment with their own spirit, their energy often shows me that they are at war with themselves. A disconnection from the spirit can feel like you're living your life on autopilot or you're not feeling fulfilled while you unsuccessfully fight for what you *think* you should be doing. Journeying to the spirit within brings clarity and peace. A connection with spirit won't mean that you will always know what to do, but it does offer you an internal place to explore. Additionally, it offers you the inner peace and knowing that you are never alone and that guidance is always available. The ability to move beyond the physical world and have access to your inner intuition, psychic ability and spirit connection is your birthright.

DO IT YOURSELF

This book offers a journey towards your own connection to spirit, here and on the other side. It is written for any level of expertise. While I wrote it with the beginner in mind, I frequently return to the exercises and journal prompts in this book myself and find a new awareness each time I revisit them. We are all lifetime learners when it comes to a spiritual quest.

This book is organised into three parts: intuition, psychic ability and spirit communication (i.e. mediumship). Throughout, I define intuition as extrasensory information you receive about yourself, psychic ability as extrasensory information you receive about others, and spirit communication as the natural ability to feel, hear and see our loved ones in the spirit world. I wrote this book in three interrelated parts because I believe that one area of awareness cannot function at its maximum potential without also developing the other two.

I've included exercises and journal prompts at the end of each chapter to increase your perception and implement what you have learned. I recommend keeping a journal nearby as you read the book, to make the most of the do-it-yourself exercises throughout the book. As you get started, my best advice is to let go a little and try them out even if you think you cannot. Connecting to the mysteries of the spirit world may not look like what you thought it would, or maybe it will be exactly how you pictured it. I personally, and begrudgingly, learned that to experience something unexplainable, one has to suspend disbelief for a little while, have a little faith and take a chance on the not-knowing.

Most importantly: be kind and do not judge your progress. Your journey will be unlike anyone else's because it is yours. No matter how you travel the path to connecting to your spirit, it is my sincere hope that through the exploration of your own spirit and connection to those who have passed, you are brought a few steps closer to your true self, for healing, closure and growth. It is my greatest honour to be a small part of your journey.

INTUITION

———

CHAPTER 1

The Spirit Body

The most uncomfortable reading I have done was for my ex-boyfriend's new girlfriend, Erin. When she walked in for the reading, I had no idea who she was. I definitely didn't know Erin was Adam's new girlfriend, and she didn't know I was the ex.

I found out, because I am a psychic medium after all.

Erin was scheduled for a psychic life reading like anyone else; my 1p.m. appointment on a Wednesday. She was twenty-one, cute, very fashionable and – like me – a recent college graduate. I explained the process to her and told her I would look at her relationships, career, family and health and in exchange she could respond with a verbal 'yes' or 'no'.

In the reading, before knowing who she was, I determined that Erin was in a relationship with a tall guy, well over six feet tall. She was worried about the relationship because he would be moving soon. I continued by taking a closer look at the boyfriend, and I was instantly hit with recognition. This energy I felt was familiar. I knew it well. *Oh dear God*, I thought. *I know this guy. She's dating Adam!*

My heart stopped. I couldn't tell her. At the time, no one outside of my closest friends and family knew I was giving psychic and mediumship readings. I was so terrified anyone would find out that I even worked under a fake name. For all of these reasons and more, I was sure Adam didn't know either. We had lost touch years ago and I had carefully covered all online traces linking me to my work as a psychic medium. I was applying to medical school to study neuroscience at the time, and I knew medical schools would not be keen to enrol psychic mediums.

Deep breaths, Fleur, I told myself. *You could be wrong. Los Angeles is a huge city, the chances are slim.* I wanted to confirm that it was indeed Adam, and so I threw out some facts.

'He's got three brothers,' I said tentatively. 'Yes!' she responded enthusiastically.

My heart raced; could it really be the same Adam? I had to know. I was no longer reading psychically and out tumbled a ton of 'Adam facts' without taking a breath: 'He plays tennis and lacrosse, DJs on the side, doesn't comb his hair, and his best friend's name is Charlie. His name is Adam. Oh, and he definitely doesn't believe in mediums.'

I looked up to see Erin staring at me, stunned. 'You're amazing!' she finally exclaimed.

Now I was really in trouble; how in the world are you supposed to give an unbiased reading to your ex-boyfriend's new girlfriend *about him*? The answer is: you can't, and I hurriedly moved on to other areas of her life. When Erin left I closed the door, slumped my body on the couch and marvelled at the odds. I couldn't believe that I had known she was dating Adam just by recognising his energy *through* Erin. I had recognised his energy in my body, like a feeling, when he wasn't even in the room!

Eight years later, I know what that feeling was. I had recognised Adam's 'signal'. The vibration he emits into the world is so specific to him that I couldn't mistake it for anyone else's. I have since come to realise that everyone has this unique signal. It is your own personal radio station and it's yours for ever.

In my reading with Erin, I was familiar with this particular signal because I had known Adam for a long time. As I extended my energy out into the world to Erin's boyfriend, I found his signal. I'd felt it before, so I recognised it, in the same way you might recognise an ex-partner's voice or the way they walk from a distance.

The thing that is sending out this signal is the spirit body. Everyone, living or dead, has a spirit body and a corresponding signal. When I follow the signal back to its source, I find the spirit body. As a psychic medium, I experience the spirit body as the part of you that cannot be created or destroyed. In other words, I believe the spirit body is the origin of human consciousness. In this book when I speak about the 'spirit body' I am speaking about all the parts of you that are not your physical form. Everyone, without exception, has a spirit body and a signal that identifies them. It's your unique energy pattern; it is indestructible and eternal.

Countless cultures and philosophies have given this part of you, the non-physical part, a variety of names such as the soul, purusha, life force or qi. It is a mysterious force. Consciousness, the act and awareness of *being*, continues to confound twenty-first-century scientists. No matter how vast our knowledge of the brain, it has not yet been scientifically explained. All the same, we know consciousness exists, because we exist.

A SCIENTIFIC PERSPECTIVE

If you are familiar with mysticism and New Age thinking, it will be easy to adopt the concept that you have a spirit body that sends out a signal. However, maybe you're new to it and a bit more resistant. I understand that; energy bodies sounds far out, but give me one more paragraph to change your mind.

From a scientific perspective, you are energy. You experience yourself as solid but you are not. Each atom in your body holds 0.001 per cent solid matter and the rest – the other 99.999 per cent – is a vacuum of empty space. That space isn't really empty because that atom is full of energy; it holds an electromagnetic field. There is so much energy packed into one single centimetre of vacuum space in your body that it gives the impression, due to gravity, of being solid. While you feel solid, actually 99.999 per cent of you is energy that is vibrating and fluxing at all times. The world around you is also not solid and therefore, you have also never actually touched anything in your life. 'Touching' someone or something is when your energy, your electromagnetic field's electrons, pushes against someone else's electrons. What you feel when you touch another person is the electromagnetic force of your electrons pushing someone else's electrons away.

In short, there is no real space between anything, there is only a continuous vibration of the electromagnetic field that connects people and things. There is a continuum of energy through all space and time connecting you to people sitting next to you and even connecting you and me, even though I might be miles and miles away from you.

None of this is New Age thinking in the slightest, it's just the truth of how our bodies, planet and solar system operate. Adding a New Age lens, I believe this electromagnetic field, the energy that connects us all, can send and receive information. In other words, I see the world as composed of many spirit bodies, and they are sending out signals everywhere.

Consider that unseen communication happens all the time. People chemically communicate through pheromones, for example. We've long known that these chemicals, acting as hormones outside the body, talk to each other and affect behaviour. We also know that much of our world is invisible to us; we see less than 0.001 per cent of the electromagnetic spectrum.

I have witnessed and known from the time when I was a child that all people can communicate through energy alone. You are a spirit body and therefore you emit and receive information all day long. You are in constant energetic communication with everything around you and this does not stop when we leave the physical body. What's more, all intuition, and psychic and mediumistic ability, is a language between spirit bodies. You also have a spirit body, so you can learn this language, too.

LANDING ON A SIGNAL

My great-grandmother, Marie, was a deeply spiritual woman. I was one of thirty-two great-grandchildren, and yet Marie was insistent on seeing me when I was born. There were other great-grandchildren she'd never met, so everyone was a little confused about her desperate need to see this one. However, they obliged. This wasn't easy; she was eighty-five years old and had been battling cancer for decades. She was very weak. In the end, she travelled while lying down in the back of a car for an hour, only to have to turn around because she was not well enough to continue the drive. A second trip was attempted later, and Marie did eventually get to hold me before she passed.

Although Marie wasn't able to be physically present for my childhood, she was able to be very impactful from the other side. She single-handedly helped me live a much easier childhood as a young medium; by speaking with me from the spirit world on a daily basis, and by convincing my parents that mediumship was real.

Great-grandma Marie regularly appeared with my great-grandfather Harry. When I was seven, I saw them with my physical eyes. Looking back, they appeared daydream-like to me, but from my child mind's perspective, they looked very real.

When they visited, they just wouldn't stop talking, and they would bicker for hours. Often they didn't even pay any attention to me. I didn't know who these two were, and they were annoying me. One day, while my mum was putting her makeup on in the bathroom for a date night with my dad, I told her I would like these two people to stop talking.

She was applying the finishing touches of blusher and asked me what they looked like. I described a tall woman and a fat short man and said, 'They won't stop arguing!' This got her attention; later she told me that it was so like her grandparents to bicker back and forth. My mum paused and asked me if I could ask their names. She recalls thinking it was funny that I stopped her by saying, 'Mum, you need to be quiet, I can't hear them if you're talking.'

After a moment, I responded with 'Marie-che' and 'Harry-ke'. These were not their names, but the nicknames they used for each other that no one else used. Marie was Marietje. Harry was Harryke. Common Dutch diminutives. Prior to this, not only did I not know their nicknames, but I hadn't even known their names. Harry, especially, had been gone for over fifty years and his name and nickname had not been used for decades.

Although she had always known I was different, my mum marks this as the moment that she understood that something very real was going on. My parents have always been supportive. They didn't encourage my mediumship, but they also didn't discourage it. Within my house, it was an open and welcomed topic. Outside of it, we didn't talk about it.

In those early days, the spirit people were seemingly sometimes there and sometimes not. I now know that they were actually always there and I would notice them when I randomly tuned to their signal. Every person in the spirit world has a signal, so communication with the spirit world is the act of attuning your spirit body to the right signal. In my experience, the majority of people also randomly land on these signals from time to time. This will appear as a random psychic thought or a moment when they sense someone in the spirit world. They aren't tuning in to the signal deliberately, it just happened that they landed on the right signal, or radio station, in that moment.

I didn't always know how to find a signal. This meant that initially my mediumship was all over the place, and my childhood spirit visitors showed up when they wanted to. I didn't know I could tune myself to a specific signal, so I had no control over it.

Perhaps you yourself have caught glimpses of the other side, or had moments of clear intuition and wondered why it isn't always there. When you don't know what radio station to dial into to get the right signal, sometimes you find it and sometimes you don't. This book will teach you how to receive and tune in to the signal at will.

THE SPIRIT BODY IS ETERNAL

I offer two kinds of readings; the distinction is which signal I am tuning in to. In a psychic life reading, I am tuning in to my client's signal and corresponding spirit body. In a medium spirit communication reading, I am tuning in to my client's deceased loved one's signal and corresponding spirit body. In both cases, my spirit body is connecting to a spirit body that emits a signal, whether here or on the other side.

When you eventually cross over to the other side, the thing that is crossing is your spirit body. I believe that the core of this spirit body doesn't change when you cross over. I have Dana to thank for this initial discovery because I was able to read for her twice. Once in a psychic life reading when she was alive, and again through spirit communication after she had passed.

The first reading took place in 2016; she made an appointment for a psychic reading and asked me to take a look at her life. As I located her signal and connected to her spirit body, it was evident that Dana was vivacious. I also felt that she had been fighting colon cancer for two years. She was up to fifty chemo treatments and I was amazed by her. Despite it all, she had started multiple charities, was raising two beautiful children, and was a public advocate for the fight against cancer. Dana's energy body and signal made an impression on me.

Two years later, Dana had passed, and I was contacted by her husband, who desired a mediumship reading, a spirit communication.

I recognised Dana's signal instantly, just as I had recognised Adam's by reading for his girlfriend. Dana clearly no longer had a physical body, so it was the spirit body I recognised. Dana's same vibrant spirit body swooped in and shared all she had seen. She spoke about what her kids were doing, the memorial, and how she was dancing, something she had loved to do here in the physical world. It was the same vivacious signal I had felt when I had met her in 2016.

Dana's memories, physical lifetime and current existence in the spirit world were all contained within her energy body. How was Dana able to communicate to me the aspects of her life, such as her love of dancing? When you cross over, your energy body won't verbally speak. Dana wasn't whispering these things into my ear – it would be much easier if she did but that's not how it works. However, this doesn't make communication impossible; it just requires a different language, which is spoken through spirit bodies.

THE BRAIN VERSUS THE SPIRIT BODY

All psychic and mediumship communication happens from one spirit body to the other. The first thing I must do when I connect is to find the right signal, the right radio station. In my experience, the ability to focus and then fine-tune in to a specific spirit body's, any spirit body's, signal is what makes someone a good psychic medium. Over the years my ability to tune in to the signal has sped up, and I translate quickly. I instantly see an image, hear a word, sense a feeling or think a thought.

Tuning in to a spirit body's signal is similar to finding a radio station. As is the case with a radio tuner, if the station is at 92.5 you may still hear static music if you're dialled in at 92.3. The music just won't be as clear. Learning to differentiate between spirit bodies is a lifelong practice for a medium. It's a difficult practice to get the radio station just right and then have enough energy to hold on to the connection without moving back into the static. Working as a medium for strangers can be difficult because you have to learn to find every signal that has ever existed.

In a reading, my spirit body receives the information, and in order to speak out loud what I am seeing, hearing or feeling, my brain takes a millisecond to process it. I am aware of this. There is a brief moment where my brain acknowledges information before I say it out loud. This can best be compared to reading a book. As you're reading these words right now your brain is transforming seemingly meaningless black lines into letters, which turn into thoughts, concepts, and maybe even visual images. It's rapid-fire. Your brain has learned to automatically create meaning out of these black lines. I have learned to translate information contained within the signal of the spirit body in the same way. At times, you may stumble across a word and have to go back. It's the same for me; if I'm moving too quickly I can lose the meaning, miss something important, or have to go back and reinterpret.

I have always experienced my brain to be an active part of this reading process – with one exception. A few years ago, I had a minor surgery in which I had to go under anaesthesia for three hours. If you've ever come out of anaesthesia, you know the feeling of waking up groggy and disoriented.

When I woke up, a kind nurse was tending to me on my left, and in that moment I had the overwhelming need to tell her that her mother was there. Everything about that reading felt different, and the information did not come into my mental space like it usually does.

In this post-anaesthesia event, this moment of thinking or translating seemed non-existent. I did not see images, feel emotions or hear words. There was no deliberate translating. I simply felt the urge to speak, and information came out. My brain didn't seem to be thinking at all, and I didn't know what I was going to say before I spoke it out loud. The information was simply there.

I moved my hand a few times to get my nurse's attention. With a lot of difficulty but an overwhelming need to speak, I managed, 'Your mother is Filipino.'

My nurse looked up, surprised, and responded, 'Yes, she was. That's weird that you would say that; even Filipino people always think I look Korean!'

I didn't have much energy, and I wanted her to stop talking. I waved my hand again to quiet her, and managed to say that her mum was there, she wanted to say hi to all nine of her children, especially Linda, and that she loved them and wanted to remind her daughter of her Filipino heritage. The information tumbled out of my mouth before my brain – a brain that felt very groggy – could catch up. I fell into a deep sleep once again. When I woke up, three nurses stood at the foot of my hospital bed. 'What do you see around me?' one asked eagerly.

When I recovered, I found myself incredibly intrigued by this experience. It was unusual because unlike my normal way of working, I didn't see images, hear sounds, or have any feeling or emotion to translate. My nurse's mother was able to connect her spirit body to mine, and the information just tumbled out of my mouth.

It also pointed to something larger, the origin of the information itself.

When I first started to offer readings, I was very concerned that my brain was just making it up. It bothered me that in a conscious state my brain would always be involved in some capacity and I would never read without bias. What was interesting about this anaesthesia experience is that it seemed to give me an opportunity to read without my conscious brain involved in the same way.

I did a little research on anaesthesia and learned that it impairs the ability of neurons to create functional connections in the prefrontal cortex, meaning the neurons can't talk to each other. Anaesthesia most strongly affects the prefrontal and parietal cortices. The prefrontal cortex is the part of the brain that differentiates between thoughts and draws conclusions. The parietal cortex processes sensory information, interprets visual information and processes language. With the remnants of anaesthesia still present, it seems my brain was massively delayed in its ability to process any images, sounds, or feelings I had. Nonetheless, I was able to communicate specific facts from the spirit world with increased ease.

This experience made me reflect on the origin of psychic and mediumship information. It emphasised for me that it is my spirit body, not my brain, that has initial access to the spirit world. Although I recognise that in intuition or psychic work the brain is processing (in most cases), I ultimately don't believe these experiences are *created* by the brain. Rather, they arise from the spirit body and are communicated through the signal and justified and further interpreted by the brain. The brain is involved to help interpret the information and can show us a picture or give a feeling, but information originates in the spirit body. The brain wants to be involved, so it is, but all communication is ultimately done from a purely energetic space, spirit body to spirit body.

That last sentence is perhaps the most important point in this book, so I will repeat it: *All energetic communication travels from spirit body to spirit body*. Understanding this concept will be the foundation for understanding how your intuition and your psychic and spirit communication skills can be used and expanded at will.

CAN YOU DO IT?

The good news is you've got a spirit body, which gives you access to your intuition and allows you to receive psychic information and connect to your loved ones in the spirit world. Everyone has a spirit body, so everyone can connect. However, if you are like most people, your mental mind often throws out the interpretation before it can even be acknowledged or voiced out loud. Or even more commonly, perhaps your brain makes you aware of the information, but because it seems odd or irrational, you dismiss it only to exclaim later, 'I knew I shouldn't have . . .!'

When I am asked if anyone can be a psychic medium, I respond that it is like dancing. Anyone can learn to dance, but not everyone will be a prima ballerina. In a similar manner, I don't believe everyone needs to be a psychic medium. The world needs people attuned to their own gifts in all areas of life. While you may not get to the point of doing readings for strangers, I have no doubt you can find the switch to turn your radio on and the volume up.

If you are a person who feels that you have never been intuitive, have never felt a spirit loved one, or have never sensed a single thing – even so, you are a naturally intuitive being. There is no way not to be one. It is your natural way of being, and you've got all the equipment.

THE FIRST STEP

I can't promise you will be able to do readings for strangers when you finish reading this book, but I do know that you can gain more intuitive insights about your own life, feel your loved ones on the other side, and learn to pay attention to the psychic information available in your environment. It all starts at home with your own spirit body. All information will be processed through it. You may have forgotten that you have a spirit body because your physical body has taken precedence. It has taken all of your attention because that physical body is the part of you that you can see, touch and hear. Your reality revolves around it and all of your judgements have been made in response to the external environment your physical body has come into contact with.

In order to be a person who is aware of intuitive, psychic and mediumistic information you have to give your spirit body an opportunity to be present within your life. This shift is an easy one, it is merely an acknowledgement. Spend some time each day closing your eyes and locating the part of you that feels like a spirit body, instead of merely a physical form.

In my classes and on my website I have a meditation exercise that will help you to shift your awareness from the mental mind into the spirit body. For most people, when they close their eyes and scan their body they land on the heart or solar plexus as the area that they feel most strongly resonates with 'being a spirit body'. I like to walk my eyes down and think of myself as seeing the world through my heart instead of my physical eyes. Instantly, I begin to perceive the world in a new way. When you close your eyes and land in your heart you can begin to think of yourself as a spirit body.

I love contemplating what we *don't* see and hear in the world. Radio waves, mobile phone signals and wifi exist all around you, but you don't see them. Although you may feel that your vision shows you a wide range of colours, you really see less than 0.01 per cent of the electromagnetic spectrum. Flies see more colours than humans do! Dogs can hear double the frequency that we can. Imagine if we could see all of the signals each spirit body emits into the world and consider that signals can travel (recall that Adam was not in the room with us when I recognised his signal).

Close your eyes and visualise yourself surrounded by these signals and the information they hold. Reimagine a conversation you've just had from the perspective of a signal exchange. Next, imagine yourself walking down a busy street with everyone's spirit bodies and signals scattered around you. Lastly, think of someone who is located far away from you. If energy can travel without the limits of time and space, can you visualise your signal extending out towards them?

It is likely that you have never considered what your spirit body comes into contact with on a daily basis. While it is simple, these practices are the perfect place to begin your journey to using your intuition, your psychic abilities and your ability to communicate with the spirit world. It offers you a shift of awareness to your internal awareness.

Your mental mind will instantly want to get involved but this is not a cerebral exercise. The mind is not the *origin* of intuition, psychic and mediumistic connection. None of this work can be done solely from the mind. You have to feel yourself as a spirit body first, and get out of your own rational way. This will be a foreign experience for you, because our twenty-first century is fixated on processing through rational thought rather than through feeling.

Shifting your awareness from your rational awareness to feeling your spirit body is a practice. You're going to have to practise it because daily life will naturally take you right back to your mental mind, which is focused on the external feedback you receive from the world. You lose the ability to be intuitive when you prioritise the external feedback of the world over your own inner feedback.

The great news is, no matter for how long it has been ignored, you innately have a spirit body. It has been working for you with or without your conscious awareness. Bringing conscious attention to the signals you are connecting to daily will give you the opportunity to be a more intuitive person, receive psychic insights and open up to your loved ones in the spirit world at will, rather than through happenstance.

DO IT YOURSELF

1. Today go about your day like you normally would and on occasion, think about yourself as a spirit body in communication with your environment. You may want to set a timer for a few times a day, to remind yourself to check in.

2. Take a moment to think about the five most important people in your life. As you focus in on each one, do they feel different in your body? Pay attention to the subtle differences and where they appear in your body.

3. Close your eyes and meditate. Think of someone you miss who lives far away. Spend some time in quiet contemplation. Recall what you feel like in their presence, what you love about them and what you would wish to say to them right now. (If they are connected to their intuition, it is likely they will reach out in some way in response).

4. Practise feeling energy fields by having someone place their hands in opposition of yours without touching each other, as if you are going to give a high-five but with both hands. Close your eyes and sense what that feels like. Try it with a few people and see if you can notice that everyone has a slightly different energetic atmosphere. With careful attention, you will be able to feel the differences in the spirit body of each person.

CHAPTER 2

Unexpected Intuition

I woke up for the third day in a row with a nagging feeling to *buy really good medical travel insurance.* I was travelling through Cambodia, and it had been a peaceful, easy solo journey. I was nearing the end of my trip when an inner call came to buy that insurance. At first, I waved it off. Yet each morning as I woke up, the feeling was strong, and my inner voice was crystal clear. *Buy really good medical travel insurance.* Notably, the message came without fear. It was simply a passing thought, seemingly out of nowhere, but remarkably, it showed up three days in a row.

While all was peaceful in the Cambodian countryside, I spent the morning purchasing the grandest travel insurance I could find. It seemed a little excessive, covering me medically for up to two million dollars! When I doubted, a pang of 'do it' went through me; so I purchased it and went about my day.

Two days later, I found myself lying in a Cambodian emergency room. I had been in a terrible car accident; my legs were covered in blood, and my actual kneecap was showing. Buying medical travel insurance didn't seem so silly any more. I was certainly glad I listened, and the scar on my leg will remind me to never doubt my inner voice again.

Which raises the question, *what* was I listening to?

Whether you call them vibes, gut feelings or intuitions, I believe they're all referring to the same phenomenon: the moment your spirit body communicates information to your conscious mind.

Intuition is always about *you*. This distinguishes it from psychic information, which is about other people. Your intuition has you at the centre. It holds information about you within your environment – you in relationship to other people, your home, your family, your diet, your career choices and your safety. Intuition always involves you in some way or another. In contrast, psychic information is knowing something about someone else that has nothing to do with you.

Intuitive information is *not less* important or specific than psychic information; it is simply different information.

Your spirit body is in a constant state of communication with your environment. Your spirit body acts as a sponge and as you go about your day, the spirit body receives information from the environment, from your interactions with others, and from universal knowledge.

Intuition happens the moment your spirit body alerts your rational mind and says 'pay attention!'

Your spirit body doesn't just absorb information, you also spread it. Your signal is beaming into your environment and the environment will also absorb some of *your* information in return. Have you ever walked into a room after people have had an intense fight and felt it in the air? Our environments absorb all of our experiences. Some of the information is held for long periods of time, which will make people feel like places are haunted. All people and places hold impressions and your spirit body gathers it all up throughout the day like a sponge, sifting through it to decide which of it is important to you.

In order for your intuition to work, your spirit body doesn't just have to gather it up, the information has to be recognised by you so that you can take action. In this process, your physical body is always the bridge. Intuition speaks through your body in feelings, physical sensations, thoughts, dreams, visions or emotions. Intuition happens when your spirit body is successful at getting the attention of your rational mind by bridging the physical body.

OVERTHINKING OVERRIDES INTUITION

Back in the United States, as I recounted the story to friends, the response was, of course you would have gotten insurance two days prior; leave it to the psychic medium. Yet the truth is, there are times when I haven't followed my intuition. A few days before the Cambodia accident happened, I called a friend and said I thought I should go home early. 'Aren't you having fun?' he asked, and I had to concede that I was. All the same, I couldn't shake the inner call to go home. I tried to rationalise the feeling away. My enjoyment of the trip completely clashed with the feeling in the pit of my stomach that I shouldn't be in Cambodia any more. I had less than a week left – I still had a list of temples to visit and restaurants I hadn't eaten at. That night, I rationally decided that changing my flights and leaving early was costly and illogical. I should stay put and enjoy my time.

Perhaps the most frustrating experience intuitive people can have is a version of 'I intuitively knew that I was walking into something unpleasant, and I overrode it and walked into it anyway.' Overthinking overrides intuition. Had I listened to my initial intuitive knowing, I could have left Cambodia and avoided the accident entirely.

UNDIRECTED VERSUS DIRECTED INTUITION

My Cambodia experience is an example of intuition I call *undirected intuition*. This kind of intuition can seem random and out of the blue. Undirected intuition finds you without being called in; it is consciously unintentional and therefore seems to just happen. It differs from *directed intuition,* which is intuition you call upon at will, for example in a meditation.

In Cambodia, I had just woken up and I was therefore in a receiving state for undirected intuition. In a receiving state, your mind isn't occupied and you're open to the subtlety of information your spirit body has been collecting like a sponge without your awareness.

In order for the intuition to rise up, the thinking brain has to take a backseat. Your spirit body could be collecting intuitive information all day long, but it has to get your attention to be of any use. It is while you are in receiving mode that the information previously hidden from you can bubble up to the surface to become available. As it bubbles up to the surface it has to activate your physical body and introduces itself through gut feelings, intuitive thoughts or visions.

The intuitive insights that seem to pop into your awareness out of nowhere may seem random, but they really aren't as rogue as they seem. If you look back at moments of undirected intuition in your life, you'll realise you were doing something that gave you the free mental space to receive. This is often a repetitive task or a moment that disengages your thinking brain such as driving, waking up from sleep, doing the dishes or exercising. These are all examples of tasks that put you into receiving mode. There are other ways too, such as standing under the shower. The way you best disengage your rational mind will be unique to you.

SURVIVAL, PEOPLE AND THINGS WE LOVE

Even when you are in receiving mode, you'll only receive a very small fraction of the information your spirit body has been constantly scanning and absorbing. If you had access to all of it, that would be entirely too overwhelming. You naturally filter out the vast majority of the information you gather up and only a very small amount will bubble up to the surface to get your attention. The information that gets to your rational brain is information you have previously established as important. This importance is measured not only by what you consciously focus on, but also through what you have deemed important subconsciously. Across the board, most people have fixed their intuitive attention to information concerning their survival, who they love and what they love.

The spirit body's most prominent point of attention is survival. I have heard incredible stories when it comes to intuitive moments of survival. A friend of mine woke up in the middle of the night, randomly moved her entire bed for no reason and woke up again an hour later to a car crashing into the house. The driver had lost control and his car went right through her bedroom wall. The car landed where her bed had stood only an hour earlier. Similarly, when asked to look back at her intuitive experiences, my student Cindy wrote, 'there have been two or three car incidents where I have been in an accident or almost, and I literally started screaming well before I should. The scream was far too advanced to be in response to the accident.'

These experiences are directly tied to life or death, but survival intuition can also take the form of choosing who you want to sit next to and who you wish to be near. Your spirit body canvasses any area you enter and reports back to you. Where you choose to sit or who you choose to speak to is never entirely random.

I once received an email from two ladies who had come to see me perform in a theatre show. While standing in the queue for the bathroom they discovered that they had identical stories of loss. Both ladies were hoping to connect to their father and son that night, and as they chatted they realised they could be twins. When one revealed another part of their grief story, the other would answer, 'Me too!'

They emailed to tell me they are best friends now. I see this time and time again at shows and in classes. People who hold similar stories of trauma always happen to sit next to each other. This is not a coincidence. When you walk into a room your spirit body is scanning and absorbing. If you are available, your survival intuition can report back to you to indicate, 'sit here, this person can help you heal.'

Intuition about who we love is seen in families, between friends, and in romantic partnerships. This is the kind of undirected intuition that tells you someone will call you, or if someone you love is in trouble or having a hard day. It defies time and space; the person could be miles away from you when out of nowhere their face comes to mind or you find yourself randomly thinking of them. Undirected intuition about people we love is also seen in the incredibly intuitive bond between parents and their children. Randomly thinking of someone can seem normal, but you know it is the intuition at work when it is followed by a call from that person or you later hear something was wrong at that point.

I once was very sick many miles from anyone and with a non-working phone. When I was able to switch my phone on, tears sprang in my eyes as I saw multiple messages come in. My mum texted that she woke in the middle of the night worried about me, and her message was followed by two missed calls from friends who had felt in that moment that they should check on me. I must have been reaching out to people energetically and they got the message. Our energetic tethers reach much farther than we can see. Just like mobile signals travel on electromagnetic waves across the world, your spirit body can also absorb information from miles away.

This phenomenon is what my friend Mikey calls 'the web'. We were joking around one day about ex-girlfriends and ex-boyfriends and how they always seem to just know when you've started dating someone new. 'I haven't received a text from her in months!' he exclaimed. 'I go on a new date, and ping! There she is.' In this case, his ex-girlfriend's spirit body still has a tether remaining that ties her to Mikey, and her intuition cares to alert her that he is moving on.

Intuition is also focused on what we love; our passion, purpose, work and hobbies. This can feel like a flash of intuitive insight. When I was a child, my mother would often remind us that in 1965, Paul McCartney heard a tune in a dream, and it was so unlike any he had written that he thought he'd stolen it. He played it for anyone who would listen, and no one could identify it. The Beatles recorded it and titled it 'Yesterday'.

This undirected intuition doesn't only exist in the arts. Professor of engineering John Mihalasky conducted intuition tests on CEOs and discovered that of those with high intuition scores, 81 per cent doubled their businesses in five years versus 25 per cent of CEOs with low intuition scores. Steve Jobs, Bill Gates and Oprah Winfrey have all been quoted praising their intuition. Even Albert Einstein said, 'The intuitive mind is a sacred gift, and the rational mind is a faithful servant. We have created a society that honours the servant and has forgotten the gift.'

Each one of these people received undirected intuitive information about the information they placed importance on. The exes of the world will care if you've moved on if they are hoping you haven't. Paul McCartney placed great importance on his art. CEOs spend their days thinking of their business and so the intuition follows suit.

Many people want to be intuitive with intention, yet I would encourage you to appreciate this undirected intuition. The intuition that seems to randomly flow into your life is powerful. You have already set your preferences by how you live your life and what you place importance on. Your spirit body is able to identify this information for you, so allowing the intuition to flow in naturally opens the door to insights you may have never thought to look for. You don't always rationally know what you need to be intuitive about.

UNDIRECTED INTUITION SPEAKS IN PATTERNS

When undirected intuition bubbles up into your awareness, it doesn't do so without order. The way information presents itself to you is a very personal and unique experience. The pathway or the bridge that intuitive information takes to get your attention is not going to be the same for you as it is for me, or for anyone else. But whatever your bridge looks like, it is well travelled. In other words, the way your spirit body speaks to you will be similar every time. I call this your *pattern*.

These patterns can be intuitive emotions, thoughts, sensations, and even visions. When intuitive information is transmitted from your spirit body to your physical body, it will choose the path of least resistance and go the same route time and time again. Even if you don't recognise yourself as holding these patterns right now, through personal enquiry and reflection on your past experiences you will see that you have them.

Finding the pattern of your intuition is an inside job. Only you can do that. No two people will operate in the exact same way.

The key to this work is that your intuition pattern will always be different from the manner in which other thoughts, emotions and visions arise within you. A journal I created, titled *Ten Minutes to Intuition,* can help you find yours.

Intuition isn't always exciting, but that doesn't make it less useful. Recently, I was driving to a meditation class and I was running late. Although one would hope to have a calm mind when entering a meditation class, my mental chatter on that night was more along the lines of, 'I'm late; how late is too late? Have they started? Can I sneak in? I really should have accounted for rush-hour traffic.' It's a mental exercise most people are too familiar with, and we all know it to be repetitive and predictable.

The fixed, mental 'I'm late' pattern I had in my mind was a repetitive worrying pattern. It was predictable and went through the same worries over and over again. It's easy to see that none of this thinking loop is intuitive. The emotions accompanying it are equally predictable – an increased heartbeat, sweaty palms and muscle tension.

As I was driving, my worried, repetitive thinking was interrupted by a new thought that came out of the blue: 'Class is in the back room today.' That was all. 'What?' I asked myself. That *other* voice remained quiet, however. My rational brain ran to question it. *It's very unlikely,* my mind responded. *I've been going to this class for two years, every Tuesday night. It has always been in the same front room, and we received no prior notice that it had changed.*

I parked and walked to the door, but was quickly stopped in my tracks because the lights were off, and I had arrived at what was clearly an empty room. Laughing at myself, I walked to the back room I'd never visited before and found everyone just getting started. Although it was certainly a random intuitive moment, it was a helpful bit of knowledge because I believe I would have left and gone home otherwise, thinking class was cancelled.

My drive to meditation may be a slightly boring example, but I use it to illustrate the difference between an undirected, intuitive thought and a logic-based thought. Furthermore, it was markedly different from my repetitive, anxious thinking and my emotions differed in their location and cadence. The pattern was not the same.

INTUITION WITH CONSEQUENCE

Quiet moments of intuition like this don't hold large consequences. Whether or not you pay attention, you will not run into harm. They are great practice material. Even if you do nothing, it is interesting to note the information and then watch it all unfold and see if you are right. Knowing the pattern does matter when the outcome has a consequence.

You want to know your pattern so well that when it matters, you trust yourself explicitly. Trusting yourself means you won't always know if you were right, because the very point could be to avoid a situation.

My best friend Kristen recently gave birth to twins and because they were born prematurely, they had to spend a few scary weeks in the NICU at the hospital. Kristen is naturally intuitive, but her mother's instinct maximised her innate knowing. Whenever anything was wrong with the boys, Kristen knew even before the many monitors showed it. The doctors were amazing, but they didn't have Kristen's intuition and I truly believe she helped her boys to health much faster than if she hadn't trusted herself. In these moments, there is no time to wait to fact-check yourself.

THE END GOAL

Through trial and error, I know my own intuitive patterns. I have learned that I can always trust my intuition when I get an out-of-the-blue thought with no emotion attached to it. This was the case in Cambodia when the thought came to 'get travel insurance', and in my car on the way to meditation class. I didn't wake up knowing my patterns and the way my intuition speaks to me overnight. The process of noticing patterns requires self-enquiry and a look back at how your body and mind have responded in the past. To find my patterns I made a list of all my intuition moments and looked back at the emotional, physical and mental quality of the experience.

Through teaching hundreds of students I have found that people primarily receive information through emotions and thoughts. It is certainly not limited to these two and I invite you to broaden the scope of your own awareness to include dreams, visions and physical sensation as well. The intuition is always unique to you.

I have compiled the most common ways the intuition presents itself when it comes to thoughts and emotions, but these are certainly not universal rules. Intuitive thoughts show up neutral. They do not have emotion attached to them, and will be emotionally different from your current state. If it is a thought, it is a one-time thought. Intuitive thoughts never come twice in one moment; they may show up again a day later (as happened for me in Cambodia) but never the exact same thought twice in that moment. You can't recreate or drum up the thought in the same way. It flashes through the mind without you being able to pause or slow it down. If you rethink and recreate the contents of the thought, the words will have a markedly different characteristic to how they entered and exited your mind the first time.

Intuitive emotions are generally found deep inside the solar plexus or the sacral area, otherwise known as the gut. While an intuitive emotion can exist around an event or a person, it will never be an angry, triggered response. The intuition never shows up as anger or hate. Similar to intuitive thoughts, you cannot recreate the intuitive emotion. Unlike other emotions, intuitive emotions can not be shifted through a good cry, a heart-to-heart or other release of emotion. They exist on a deeper plane.

WISHFUL THINKING, IMAGINATION, ANXIETY AND PREJUDICE

Intuition doesn't live in a vacuum. Non-intuitive emotions and thoughts exist too, of course. Physiological and emotional responses go through the same five senses as intuition does. They all must be processed through the physical body, so it is no surprise that the intuition can get lost or confused with wishful thinking, imagination, anxiety or prejudice. These non-intuitive emotions and thought patterns are characterised by heightened emotions, fear, nervousness and daydreaming, so are easy to initially think of as intuition.

But, they are not the same. With careful attention to your own emotions, you'll begin to see that your body holds repetitive, and therefore predictive, responses to what you experience. An intuitive thought, emotion or sensation simply won't look or feel the same or hold the same wording, emotion or pattern as the worry, anxiety, imagination or prejudice. If the two look and feel similar, it is not intuition.

While not everyone who has anxiety will experience the same symptoms, their own anxiety symptoms will often be repetitive. You will also find that you have triggered responses to certain situations. We tend to hear about triggers through big trauma experiences, and these are certainly ones to note. However, they can also be slight and unnoticed by you, such as racial prejudice.

Prejudice is reactionary and never intuitive. Non-intuitive reactions often correspond to a person, place or thing that triggered your response, whereas the intuition more often comes in times of peace. In order to know how your intuition speaks to you, you have to take a look at the ways in which it doesn't.

Finding your pattern is most easily accessible by observing past behaviour. Take some time to find the moments in which you can identify feeling wishful thinking, imagination, anxiety and prejudice. We will all have experienced these emotions at one time or another. By reflecting back on them, you can begin to identify how and where they show up in your body and awareness. I know that my worrying thoughts come with a racing, anxious feeling in my body. They are always in response to a current or upcoming event such as a conversation or meeting. I have a physiological response and my chest feels constricted. I am jumpy. I am often emotional and things easily make me cry when I have anxiety. These experiences are very different from the cool and collected thoughts and feelings I get when it is my intuition.

Similar to reflecting back on non-intuitive emotions, the starting point of all intuitive work is then to take a look at how we distinguish a normal, rational thought from an intuitive thought, from a non-intuitive triggered response. By comparing the intuitive with the non-intuitive you can distinguish and differentiate between these emotional states and thoughts.

I wish I could tell you exactly how *your* intuition pattern works, but this is impossible. Only you can do that. In my *Ten Minutes to Intuition* journal, the first step I ask people to take is to reflect on their past intuitive moments. Some of these instances are relatively small, such as thinking of a friend right before they call. Others are connected to the larger decisions of life. When I do this initial exercise with my students, they often reflect back that most of their biggest life choices: career, moves, marriages – all hold instances of intuitive moments. No matter the size or complexity of the intuitive moment, I ask them to list how, where, when, and in what manner their intuition appeared. You can also do this on your own. Over time, you'll find that your intuition holds a pattern too.

If your intuition seems to have a weird component, you're not alone. For example, when my mum says something that is predictive and true, she gets goosebumps on her body. Knowing your pattern, no matter what it is, is the key to future intuitive success.

The next time it appears, you won't have to wonder. You'll know you can trust it. As with any good relationship, trust is built by repetition. When the intuition has repeatedly delivered good results, you can trust it.

LOSS OF TRUST: INEFFECTIVE UNDIRECTED INTUITION

In my Cambodia ER adventure story, I described two types of undirected intuition: a feeling about leaving Cambodia that I ignored, followed by an inner call to buy insurance that I did not ignore.

Neither of these intuitive instances were asked for or called upon, and this is what makes them undirected. However, even though I didn't listen to the first, both got my attention. The information my spirit body had absorbed about an upcoming injury in Cambodia was important enough to be brought to the surface in my rational brain, and *I noticed it*. I just didn't trust it.

Distrusting what the spirit body is telling you is a common way for intuition to get lost. The information made it from your environment to your spirit body, it was then brought to the surface, and you had an emotion, thought, sensation or vision. It went through all of that to be ignored.

This result is often followed by the cry, 'I knew I shouldn't have!'

When we think about it this way, it seems laughable. Your spirit body is designed for and wants to help you, and yet time and time again, you ignore it. Sometimes, the consequence is minimal. The intuitive information will find you in another way.

Other times, the consequence can be catastrophic. When you always and completely ignore your intuition, there is a strong disconnect with the inner self, or a constant inner battle. A disconnect from self can lead to depression, frustration, and the loss of inner trust.

I see this often in my clients; most people have a very set way of how they *think* their life should be, and they leave very little room for their own spirit to have a voice. Their life is lived solely focused on external feedback. They don't trust themselves, ever.

If you find you don't trust yourself, know that your spirit body will never give up on you. Your intuition is always accessible, and although giving your spirit a voice can seem scary at first, I find that doing so can give a deep sense of peace and clarity.

HOW TRUST IS LOST

Most people who don't listen to their intuition have had an experience in their past when they lost trust. For some, this happened in childhood. Children are energetically observant, and therefore distrust of your intuition frequently starts in childhood. Often parents, with obvious good intentions, tell their children everything is okay in the household even though there is a nasty divorce happening, someone is gravely ill, or there is great financial trouble. This is not restricted to parents; it can happen in any relationship.

Although children are not meant to hold the heaviness of these experiences, telling them their feelings are unwarranted and nothing is wrong can be in direct conflict with what they sense. Early on, this disrupts inner trust because external feed-back is given precedence over internal knowing. When a child's intuitive and psychic feelings of unease oppose what they are told and what they see, the intuitive compass is disrupted. Instead, acknowledging the issue to be true while assuring the child that they are safe will keep their internal compass in alignment.

It is also possible to experience this confusion as an adult. Inner trust can be destroyed in relationships that have a great deal of lying or deception; you might know this as gaslighting.

Perhaps your distrust started after a moment when you misconstrued anxiety or wishful thinking as intuition. I have worked with many women who find their intuitive trust shattered when a relationship doesn't turn out the way they wanted. However, looking back at how you perceived what you thought was your intuition, you will always find that wishful thinking presents differently.

The first step to reclaiming your ability to connect with your intuition is to recognise that you have this ability. The second step is to recognise the times in the past when you were right after all. Rebuilding your trust is the key to returning to your innate ability to recognise your intuition.

Recognising when you're right and celebrating the small moments of success will redefine your inner trust.

SIMPLY HUMAN

I don't think you should throw all logic out the door. However, it is likely you've been taught your entire life to live in the feedback of your external world and always acknowledge rationality over your intuition. If you always side with the external and continually dismiss the internal you'll miss out on what your spirit is saying every time, because a common trait of intuition is that it often doesn't match what you see with your own eyes.

Living an intuitive life doesn't mean the pendulum has to swing away from the rational world. There can be balance. A simple acknowledgment of what you received is all it takes.

When you invite intuition to the table, everything can change. Giving your intuition room to speak, a chance to be heard and to be considered without immediate dismissal, marries your internal world with your external reality. While the rational brain will get the last word at times, other moments allow intuition to lead the way and prove to you that it works on your behalf.

Nor should you view the intuitive journey as the path to a 'perfect' life. Even when you listen to your intuition, there will be times in your life when your guidance system feels misplaced. Perhaps your intuition guided you into a relationship and then it guided you out of it. Your logical brain may analyse these choices and say, 'What a waste of time, if it didn't last why would I have entered it?' This points to a fallacy that an intuitive life is a life in which you avoid all hard things.

You need these moments of discomfort to know what you want and to access your internal power and strength. Not to mention, many of life's greatest joys come to be because of a difficult circumstance.

An intuitive life is not a life in which you are protected from human experience; quite the opposite. An intuitive life is a life in which you are guided into the most expansive version of yourself, and at times that will include perceived failure and new beginnings. When we have experiences we don't like, we have the opportunity to more clearly define what we do like. Without failure we would not know what we wish to create and what we wish to be more intuitively aligned with.

I can promise you that I and other psychic mediums, no matter how well established and amazing in their many gifts, don't know everything that is going to happen in our own lives, nor is that the goal. I wouldn't ask that you make it your goal either. First of all, there is way too much intuitive and psychic information in the world to sift through it all. Secondly, none of us are saints; we are human.

An intuitive life is a life in which you are connected with your spirit to live the most expansive reality, not the socially deemed 'perfect' reality. It is not your intuition's job to make your life easy – it can make it easier, but that is not its ultimate goal. Instead, it is the intuition's job to constantly and incessantly guide you back home to your spirit body core, the most expansive part of you that has always existed and will always exist. It guides you back because at the core of your spirit you desire to fulfil your purpose and reach your true potential.

DO IT YOURSELF

Inventory:

Take inventory of the moments in your life when your spirit body 'spoke up'. Don't forget to include your childhood. Choose three intuitive moments in your life or moments in which you sensed the spirit world around you. Answer the following questions:

1. How did the information show itself? Was it a dream, a feeling, a knowing?
2. Where did you feel it in your body? Be specific. It may help to reimagine yourself in that moment and relive it.
3. How could you recognise the information if it showed up again?
4. For each event, recall what your physical environment was like.
5. For each event, recall what you were doing when you received the information (driving, washing dishes, waking up, painting, etc.).

Simply giving your spirit body a voice will tell your mental mind to pay attention. By repetitively doing the above exercise, you'll begin to see that your spirit body has been speaking to you this entire time. It is time to give it a seat at the table.

Non-intuitive thoughts and emotions:

The starting point of all intuitive work is to distinguish wishful thinking, imagination, anxiety or prejudice from an intuitive thought.

1. Begin by locating a worry you have had in your mind. Revisit all the thoughts you have on this topic; it can be easier to write them down. Take a look at where these thoughts sit inside your body. Then, notice if they have an emotion attached. Ultimately, you will run out of thoughts, emotions and locations about this topic, and will land right back on the ones you've already had. There will be a pattern.

2. Repeat the above exercise for anxiety, wishful thoughts, imagination and prejudice.

Compare and contrast:

1. Identify two key differences between how your intuition patterns and your non-intuitive patterns present themselves.

2. Are there any experiences in your life that made you distrust your own intuition? How can you remind your-self now that you can trust yourself if these situations were to happen again?

CHAPTER 3

Feeling Too Much or Too Little

It is a fun challenge for me as a teacher when I am immediately and adamantly told by a new student, 'I've never been intuitive about anything.' 'Are you sure?' I'll ask. 'Absolutely,' they'll say with conviction. These students stand firmly by their lack of experiences, and I have to take them at their word. Obviously, my exercise to find patterns would do very little for these students who swear they have never felt, heard or seen anything remotely intuitive.

Aza is one of these students. He works as a professor and has a deep philosophical interest in the psychic world but lacks a practical connection to it. 'I have no ability, just curiosity,' he told me. I replied that it simply cannot be true that he has no intuitive ability. If he has a spirit body (and everyone does), then he is an intuitive being.

INEFFECTIVE UNDIRECTED INTUITION: I FEEL NOTHING

Aza has a spirit body, and it is in constant communication with the world. He is absorbing information in an undirected manner just like all of his intuitive classmates. However, in Aza's case, his spirit body is not effectively transmitting the absorbed intuitive information to his rational brain. His intuition exists but it is ineffective at getting his attention. If intuition is the moment your spirit body communicates information about you with your conscious brain, then in Aza's case, the communication bridge is not happening. He has no emotional pings, no intuitive thoughts coming into his head, no bodily sensations or clear visions. The information that normally bubbles to the surface from the spirit body isn't bubbling up at all.

I believe his spirit body still absorbs information and holds intuitive insights, but it just hasn't found the path to getting his rational mind's attention. For a successful bridging to happen, the intuition requires two things. First, a moment for the rational mind to recede into the background (through the repetitive activity we've spoken about, such as during mindfulness, exercise and sleep) and second, through embodiment.

ALL INTUITION STARTS WITH EMBODIMENT

There is a misconception that connecting to the metaphysical requires a detachment from the physical. A 'woo woo' spacey-ness, if you will. The opposite is true. The intuition, psychic awareness, and connecting to spirits are all enhanced when you anchor into the physical body. All energetic information has to travel through your physical body to get to you. There is no other pathway, no other bridge. The body is where you live and it collects energy all day long. To receive what is collected, you have to listen to the body. Your body is your messenger.

Embodiment is the practice of connecting to the inner landscape of your emotions and feeling how emotions originate and are held within your physical form. From a spirit body perspective, we can think about embodiment as aligning with our own signal.

I have learned the most about embodiment work through yoga teachers and therapists, such as my dear friend Carly Thomas, who works in both of these fields. I met Carly in Lisbon, and we immediately became fast friends. One of the reasons our friendship is so special is that we discuss spiritual topics over lunch as if we're talking about shopping or dating, which we do in equal measure. On one particular day, I was telling her about my student Aza. 'I had a client just like that,' she replied. 'He was a classified genius, and as is the case with most super intelligent people who live in their heads, came to me because he was suffering from crippling anxiety.'

To get her client embodied, she was working with holding long yoga poses while chanting. Chanting requires the breath to slow down, which relaxes the nervous system.

She asked her client what he would like to chant, offering up options such as 'om' or 'yahweh'. Instead, the man turned to her and said, 'I'd like to chant "Dave".'

She laughed as she recounted the story. 'I have to say, I'd never chanted Dave before. I had to ask him though, "Who is Dave?"'

'My dog,' he answered nonchalantly.

So Carly and her client stood side by side. In warrior pose, arms extended and legs firmly planted, chanting 'Daaaaaavee, Daaaaaave, Daaaaaave,' over and over again. All of a sudden, the man started shouting out weird calculus equations with a lot of xs and ys. Carly looked on in confusion.

He interrupted himself by shouting, 'Oh my God! I've got it!' and ran to grab pen and paper. When he was finished scribbling it all down, he told Carly that he'd been trying to solve a seemingly impossible physics problem for months, when all of a sudden, in that moment the answer dropped in. 'Dave is magic!' he exclaimed.

Carly and I both know that while Dave may very well be magic, it's the embodiment that did the trick and created the bridge from intuition (about what he loved) to his rational mind.

There are many entry points to embodiment. Chanting and breathwork are effective ways to have an internal awareness of the physical body. Another way is to isolate emotions and notice where they exist within the body.

To bridge the disconnect and get him moving towards embodiment, I started my client, Aza, off with an emotion wheel. Created by the late psychologist Robert Plutchnik, the emotion wheel describes basic emotions: bad, surprised, fearful, angry, happy, sad or disgusted. I've included it on the next page.

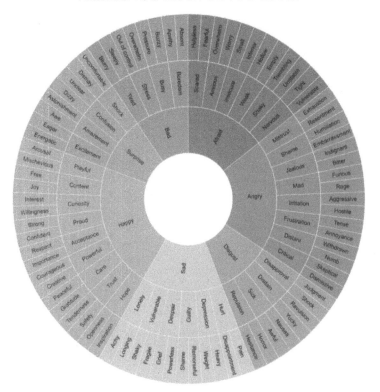

Illustration from www.dralbertwong.com/feelings-wheel/

When I ask my clients to work with the emotion wheel, we begin by having them isolate an emotion they are currently feeling. Let's say they choose 'I am feeling bad' about their job. Each basic emotion on the wheel contains degrees of each emotion. I then ask them to more specifically identify the emotion of 'bad' as 'bored, busy, stressed or tired'. When they identify this emotion as 'stressed about work', it brings them to the next layer of the emotion, which could uncover the emotions of 'overwhelmed' or 'out of control'.

The next step is to identify *where* in their body that emotion exists – for example, a lump in the throat, tightness in their chest, or a sinking feeling in the pit of the stomach.

Aza initially countered this exercise with the logical argument that not all these emotions are intuitive. He is right, of course. However, if he does not pay attention to any emotions, he will surely miss the intuitive ones, too.

Learning to identify your emotions will help you see their pattern. An intuitive emotion will exist in a different place in your body than other emotions and will arise in a different way. Embodiment is the practice of taking those emotions and isolating them to where they exist within your body and the pattern they hold. Non-intuitive emotions have patterns as well and to have effective intuition, you want to know the difference.

Expecting the intuition to be a booming voice is a recipe for disaster. Intuition speaks in subtlety. What is already within us and what exists outside of us doesn't speak in words. (If you're looking for a booming voice, stop. I only know a handful of people that's happened to, and it's an event you'll remember for ever if it does.)

Despite the subtlety, the information available is substantial. It's plentiful, and it's everywhere. All people, living and deceased, hold infinite amounts of information. All places hold infinite amounts of information. All objects hold infinite amounts of information. If you're not in a receiving state, you won't access any of it.

For this reason, intuition is easier when you're in alignment with yourself. If it's your spirit body speaking to you, hearing it will be difficult if you're at war with yourself.

Regina, a thirty-four-year-old woman in the corporate world, was at war with herself. She reached out to me for a psychic reading, and I saw that she had recently experienced a relationship with a man, the beginnings of a marriage and then an abrupt end to the marriage. She verified that she had gotten married, but that within three months the marriage had dissolved. I saw alcohol abuse in the relationship and a controlling nature in her former husband that he had witnessed in his own father. It was as if the act of marriage had set in motion all the controlling traits this man had witnessed as a child. Regina recounted that after their wedding, he told her, 'I own you.' The marriage was troubling, but what troubled Regina most was that she was incredibly blindsided. Although she had doubts at the beginning of the relationship, over time he started to seem like her forever partner. Regina didn't understand how she could have been so wrong about someone. She later told me, 'I have never felt depression like this. I see no purpose in life.'

Taking a closer look at Regina's spirit body, a few things struck me. Although Regina was in fact a very sensitive person, she had learned from an early age to put her emotions 'away'. She ran her life on logic, hard work and self-sacrifice. I saw that she gave no room for her intuition in life, no room for the emotions, and her spirit body was in complete disconnect with her physical body and rational mind. There was no room for her spirit body to get her attention.

I expressed to her what I saw: that a part of her depression stemmed from her dismissal of her inner knowing and emotions. The path forward would be to embody her feelings. I felt like dance and movement might first unlock her stored emotions and then move her towards identifying her inner knowing. She would have to work with a therapist integrated with trauma to help embody, process and release her emotions to access her intuition.

'How weird,' she said, 'I have debilitating panic attacks now, and the first panic attack happened in a dance class.'

I was not surprised; the movement had unlocked the emotions but they had not been processed afterwards, and she had only worked to dismiss them more. I expressed to her that I was sure that she could return to feeling peace, but encouraged her to seek a trauma therapist who could work with her to embody emotions through movement, and I left her with a few recommendations.

Regina's story is not unfamiliar to me. I've seen it countless times. Many people function in a world where they work in complete dismissal of their intuition and feelings. I believe it is likely that Regina experienced many emotions and intuitive nudges indicating that the relationship was not a good fit for her, but hadn't found a way to listen to herself yet. This doesn't mean she isn't capable. She has everything inside of her to begin the process of listening.

If you, like Aza or Regina, believe yourself to be completely void of intuitive ability, consider that this book made it into your hands because you were ready for it. Curiosity is all you need because the ability is already inside of you. Believing that you are an intuitive being can be a leap of faith for some. If you can suspend disbelief for even a short while, I know you will surprise yourself.

CAN ANYONE DO THIS?

It can be hard to see yourself as an intuitive being when there is no physical manifestation of the ability. When you see someone's ability to be much more heightened than your own you may believe that this means you have none. Accessing metaphysical information is a natural ability but it is also a skillset. This is true for all human ability. Let's consider the art of dancing. While it would require a heightened natural ability to become a prima ballerina, everyone can learn to dance. The intuitive, psychic and medium ability is the same. You may not go on to be a professional, but you can learn to connect.

In the western world, we see the ability to connect to the metaphysical as reserved for a select few. However, it is much more widespread as a general ability in other parts of the world.

I have travelled to India many times. I believe a great deal of the appeal of and draw to this amazing country for me is that my work is considered incredibly normal there. One morning, I was having breakfast at a hotel in Rishikesh the week before my students would join me for my annual retreat. Vivek, the hotel owner, asked if he could join me as he was curious about my upcoming retreat.

Vivek was genuinely interested in my work, not because it was unusual but because it seemed rather ordinary to him and he didn't comprehend how I could do this for a job.

'You mean, this is an unusual job in your country?' he asked, incredulous that I would be in a small minority of working mediums. He was also baffled that people in the United States could be sceptical. He pointed to the man who had just brought me my breakfast: 'You see that man who just brought us eggs? He is a medium. So is my mother, and many of my friends. So many people can do something like that.'

His comment made me laugh. Of course India has more psychics and mediums than the western world! The population is raised with yoga, meditation and spirituality deeply integrated into everyday life. While not everyone in India is a medium for others, of course, the people with a natural ability didn't have to undo years of suppressing it. I would venture to say that as a whole, intuitive intelligence is at a much higher level in the eastern world versus the western world. For this reason, my job wouldn't seem foreign to Vivek.

We can catch a glimpse of this widespread, natural ability to be metaphysically in tune when we look at children. As the phrase goes, 'Out of the mouth of babes.' Young children, unencumbered by rational, external feedback, can often be remarkably wise and pick up on the weirdest things.

It was bagel day at my office in the US. Every Friday, the secretaries provided a large selection of bagels for the whole floor. It was a real treat. On this Friday, I had a reading scheduled for a woman and her young son. As I met Ben and his mother in the lobby area, I asked him if he wanted a bagel. 'You've got to be kidding me,' said his mum with a laugh. 'This whole morning he's been saying he is going to eat a bagel today, and we never eat bagels.' He got his bagel!

I think our whole world is full of information. Most of us wouldn't include bagels on our list of 'things we love' that would allow our spirit body to alert our rational mind about bagel opportunities, but Ben did. He had not yet learned to dismiss his impulse for a breakfast bagel with the rational knowledge that his mum didn't buy them.

I FEEL EVERYTHING: INEFFECTIVE UNDIRECTED INTUITION

My student Luna was the opposite of Aza. She felt *everything*. While Aza wanted to turn his intuition radio on, Luna was desperate to turn things off. None of it was a clear radio signal, however, and it all blended together to burn her out.

Luna introduced herself to me as 'the sensitive one' in her family. She preferred to stay home, and over the years had become more and more reclusive. Luna couldn't enter crowded places without feeling instantly drained. She often felt heavy emotions that weren't her own. She couldn't distinguish between her true intuition and the feelings of other people. Intuition didn't seem like a gift to Luna at all; it seemed much more like a curse.

When someone is overly sensitive like Luna, it can feel as though all the radio stations are playing at the same time without a way to clearly tune in to any useful information.

Feeling too much is also an ineffective way for undirected intuition to work. In Luna's case, her spirit body is in a heightened state of collecting energy all day long, yet none of it is clear. Any useful information is missed because the overwhelm makes all incoming information too chaotic and intense. In these instances, it can be hard to isolate a pattern because bits of information are all crashing into each other. Feeling too much is also an indication that the intuition (insight about yourself) is getting all messed up with psychic awareness (insight about other people).

Luna had done a lot of research on the topic. She identified as a 'highly sensitive person' (HSP), a term coined by Elaine Aron, a psychiatrist and researcher. This made her feel less alone;

20 per cent of the worldwide population are HSPs. Additionally, she believed herself to be an empath (a smaller group within the 20 per cent). An empath is someone who experiences someone else's feelings within their own mind and body. She explained to me that she could feel someone's emotions even if they were hiding them, and that she could also feel others' bodily pains. Often, she confused these feelings and sensations with her own.

There is nothing wrong with being highly sensitive; it can be a real asset. When highly sensitive people are functioning at their best, their intuition is razor-sharp, effective at getting their attention without being overwhelming. Luna, however, was out of control. When too much information enters the spirit body and bubbles up to the surface without any ground rules, it can feel like holding a metal rod in a lightning storm.

Many of my highly sensitive students tell me that their lives feel outside of their control. Being around anyone puts them into overdrive. It can feel lonely and exhausting. I've seen plenty of people turn to overeating, overworking or smoking to cope with their hypersensitivity. If this sounds like you, I promise that with a little bit of work, you can shift yourself from overload into a working intuition.

BOUNDARIES

The first step is to take a look at your boundaries. When I encounter students who act as highly absorbent sponges in their environment, I always see that their energetic boundaries are incredibly porous. They let everything in. You can tell the nature of your energetic boundaries by seeing how you deal with boundaries in your physical relationships. Energetic boundaries are always mirrored in the physical boundaries you hold with people in your physical world.

Boundaries are a funny thing for sensitive people. People who can feel everyone's emotions, needs and wants recognise that on a spirit level, there are no boundaries. Thinking back on the electromagnetic fields we occupy as physical beings, we can note that there are no boundaries energetically either. Setting boundaries then often feels backwards to them. They place more importance on the unity of all people, or look towards others for the answers, rather than turning to the self.

That would be fine if everyone was in alignment with their divine spirit core at all times. But that is not the human experience. When we occupy a physical body we experience separateness, and this is an important part of functioning and existing in a physical world. Other people are divine creatures but in order to align with others at their best, we must first find our way back to the spirit within ourselves.

Boundaries call us back to the self. They work to encourage us to listen and honour our own spirit body before we pay attention to everyone else's, like the classic airline call to put your own oxygen mask on first. When we do not listen to our spirit body first, we get lost in the chaos of the world.

Luna lacked physical and emotional boundaries. She placed herself last, overworked herself to please others, and rarely took a moment to herself. She was constantly asking others what she should do, rather than turning to herself for answers. Her boundaries were fuzzy at best and non-existent at worst. Often, Luna placed a higher importance on how others felt around her than on how she felt. To get her started, I had Luna take inventory of how she allowed people to interact with her at work, school, in her family and in her friendships. She started to notice how many times in a day she felt a loss of personal power and was overwhelmed by the needs and wants of others.

I knew this first step was important, because as a highly sensitive person myself, I know boundaries are the reason I can do my work without getting overwhelmed by information every minute of the day. Strong boundaries keep me from carrying what doesn't belong to me in the first place. I have never found my intuitive, psychic or mediumship abilities to be scary because I know that I choose what I allow in no matter what. Remember, the intuitive information that bubbles up to the surface does so because you have placed interest there or have an energetic tether. We are intuitive about who we love, what we love, and about survival. You get to choose and decide for yourself what you want to receive and what you don't.

To get clear on her boundaries, I had Luna first look at the boundaries she wanted to set and strengthen in her relationships. Second, she created a contract with herself and her intuition. She wrote down the dos and don'ts of what she wished to receive and how she wished to receive it. We coupled this with a daily awareness practice around what was hers and what wasn't. Her sister-in-law's disastrous marriage? Not her depression to take on. Her boss's expectation for 24/7 availability? Time to set a new work schedule.

Intuition and psychic overload rarely happen all in one go. They are cumulative. As a sensitive person moves throughout their day, they are constantly collecting stuff. For this reason, Luna's next exercise was to take her energetic temperature throughout the day. I instructed her to set a timer for herself at least five times throughout her day, at which points she would take a brief moment to notice how she was feeling.

Luna, like many sensitive people, started noticing when her emotions and energy would shift. She'd wake up in great spirits, go to work, say hello to a colleague who loved to complain, and it would go downhill from there. When she checked in with herself at 7a.m. her mood was good; at 9a.m. it was in the dumps. The only change had been one conversation.

This is the key to handling a highly sensitive spirit body. If you're an empath, it is important to identify the times when your mood has been changed or altered. If you don't, it accumulates, and you overload. The check-in at 9a.m. allowed Luna to make a mental note that the negative feeling she had after speaking with her co-worker was not hers. Rather than assuming this heavy, negative feeling was her own and carrying it throughout her day, she was able to mentally separate it from herself.

CLEARING

Clearing your energy can be done in meditations and is often done through visualisation. I find that the clearing power isn't about what you are visualising; what is important is the intention. There are many ways you can incorporate visualisation into your boundary-setting. You can start or end your day in the shower, imagining that you are washing away all the energy that is not yours. You can visualise a bubble around you, or place mirrors in your mind's eye to reflect back anything that doesn't belong to you.

I think it is also possible to clear spaces. Your environments are absorbing and holding information about you, too. When your signal extends into your home every day, it accumulates. You then re-enter the space and often calibrate to what you left behind. It is nice at any time to exist in a cleared space. For many years, when I went back home to visit my family I would clear the house as the first thing I did. I didn't always tell them that I was clearing the house, and I loved waking up to exclamations of, 'Wow, I slept so well last night!' at breakfast the next morning. Clearing spaces isn't only for spots that feel like they have 'bad energy'; we release a lot of our emotions, stressors and interactions into our environments and often, they leave some energetic residue, which it is wise to clear out regularly. Human emotions such as grief, anger or frustration are not 'bad', and can be safely expressed to allow the nervous system to release and recalibrate. However, while you may have moved the energy of those emotions from your body, you have deposited them into your environment. At the end of your day when you go back home, you will step right back into the anger you left behind earlier. This can cause the anger to reactivate in your body, as it is easy for your own energy field to recalibrate to these 'discarded' emotions. A regular clearing of your energetic environment will help you to stay in the present moment instead of being constantly pulled back into old energetic patterns.

Clearing spaces is easy. You can do so by setting the intention to clear and visualising the environment, or by using tools and techniques like burning sage. I do not think you need sage to clear a space but I do believe the act of clearing using a tool will help you to focus on your intention. It is also possible to clear a space by filling it with a new, uplifted emotional state. You can often find me cranking up the volume of the music that makes me happy and dancing around the house. The combination of sound waves and joy clears the space, and your own spirit body, right away.

GROUNDING

Through setting boundaries and clearing her energy, Luna was able to ground herself. *Grounding* is a big word in the metaphysical community. My definition of grounding is a return to the self in body, spirit and mind. You can think of it as creating a clean space from which to work. It's hard to pay attention to a new file being placed on your desk if your workspace is covered in thousands of files scattered and falling off the edges. Similarly, it's nearly impossible to pay attention to any new piece of intuitive information if it's competing with a million others.

As the word implies, grounding can be done through physically connecting with the earth. We can theorise this process as happening in the same way that we ground electricity. We all know you can get electric shocks from electronic equipment, such as your car. At the most extreme, you'll see your hair stand straight up. We know the fastest way to get rid of this static electricity in the body is to discharge it from the body to the ground. This is as simple as, if you are outside, removing your shoes and socks and standing on the ground. Grounding balances the excess charge between the charged object and the ground.

In a similar manner, many people have found that putting their feet on the ground helps them even when they're not working with static electricity build-up. We can also bridge this to thinking about the spirit body. The practice of grounding is the practice of discharging all the excess information your spirit body has collected. Grounding is your reset button.

Grounding can be done in a physical way, outside in nature or through physical activity and exercise. It can also be done through energetic work. I find the most direct manner is to determine where your energetic attention is going. If you're a meditator, you can practise this by closing your eyes and doing a normal meditation practice first. Then, begin to pull your energy back from anything you can think of – family, friends, colleagues, clients, work, locations, the past, the future, and anywhere else you may have left it. If you're not into meditation, writing it all down can help too. Even just identifying what you're caught up in can help you release it.

This process is the act of calling yourself back home. Coming back to the centre of you. Pulling back your energetic tethers from the rest of the world. Where is your attention oriented? Where is your energy oriented? You can't work from a messy orientation. If you want to identify the important things you are intuitive about, you need to have a clean working surface. Energy flows where attention goes.

My last advice for Luna was to give herself plenty of time to relax and recharge. If you are particularly sensitive to people and places, you – more than anyone else – will have to give yourself time away from those people and places. When you're very sensitive to other people's emotions and internal struggles, personal timeouts throughout the day can make a huge difference in your quality of life. Taking time away, regardless of your sensitivity, is always useful to opening up as the intuition cannot be heard or felt without making space for it in our busy lives.

INEFFECTIVE UNDIRECTED INTUITION: WHEN GRIEF GETS IN THE WAY

The last example of ineffective intuition applies to those who have always been intuitive but find themselves in a kind of temporary fog. It is not uncommon for grief, loss, heartbreak, depression, or any other overwhelming emotion to completely block out any other subtle information. During periods of grief, people are often afraid of finding stillness; they may be afraid of what can bubble up to the surface when they do.

It may sound like a cliché, but time does heal. When you've experienced a particularly destabilising event, it can be hard to find your centre again. Intuition works through subtlety. Big emotions can blow subtle impulses out of the water completely. Your intuition has not abandoned you in these instances; it has simply taken a backseat while big emotions overshadow the subtle information your spirit body is receiving.

Rather than getting angry at yourself for not being as intuitive as you normally are, be patient and kind with yourself. For intuition to work in the most effective way, grounding and embodiment are required. Nourishing yourself in body, mind and spirit will allow you to open back up.

If the idea of opening back up feels uncertain, working alongside a therapist during periods of grief and loss can give you a safe space to welcome intuition back in. I have a regular practice of recommending that my clients seek out mental health professionals who can help them move through times in their lives that feel particularly overwhelming. No matter what, your intuition never disappears; it is simply hiding out, waiting for you to find it again.

73

DO IT YOURSELF

Do you identify as someone who feels too little or too much? If you are someone who feels too little, complete the following exercises:

1. Incorporate breathwork or mantras into a yoga practice or dance. You can get embodied in many ways so give yourself an opportunity to try a few different modalities until you find the right one.

2. Keep the emotion wheel found in this chapter on hand. Identify the exact emotions you feel throughout your day.

3. When you have labelled your emotion, identify where in your body that emotion arises. Begin to notice the differences between intuitive information and anxiety, wishful thinking, or the imagination.

If you are someone who feels too much, complete the following exercises:

1. Take an inventory of your personal boundaries. Is there an area of your life that lacks firm boundaries? This can show up in family, relationships, work, etc. How can you establish firmer boundaries?

2. Make a list of Dos and Don'ts for your intuition. The Dos are the parts of your intuition you would like to experience, such as, 'I do desire to receive emotional feedback from those around me,' and the Don'ts are experiences you would like to avoid, such as, and 'I don't want those emotions to linger so that I confuse them as my own.'

3. Set a timer throughout the day and notice if your energy has changed around certain people or places. Later, in a meditation practice, visualise yourself pulling your attention and energetic tethers back from these people and places.
4. Where can you schedule in some time to relax and recharge?

Record every intuitive moment you receive, and how you receive, it in a journal. This exercise will be the key to noticing your intuition in present time, rather than through reflection.

CHAPTER 4

Intuition on Demand

One summer, when I was ten, I had a marvellous cabin leader at summer camp. Getting all of us pre-teen girls in our own bunks and asleep at night was a heroic feat in itself, and she had an incredibly effective nightly ritual. As we lay down, she instructed us to pay attention to our bodies. Starting with our toes, she told us to scrunch them up really tight, hold, and then release. We tightened and released, bringing our attention back to the here and now. In collective mindfulness, we moved up the body and drifted into sleep. We were out.

When camp ended for the week and I was back at home, I couldn't wait to introduce my parents to this magic. I made them lie down, and I parroted back what I'd heard. I wanted them to feel the bliss. I knew it to be revolutionary.

The next time I came across this magic, I was lying on my back on a yoga mat in a college gym, legs and arms angled slightly outward. It was the final corpse pose of my first class; I was eighteen. It had been eight years, but I recognised the calm immediately. That day, I learned it was called *meditation*.

These moments were the first times I was able to play a direct role in creating a passive state. The class formed the very early stages of my meditation practice. At first, it seemed too simple to be meditation; this relaxation felt more like falling asleep. But it was a start. This start grew into my now daily meditation practice. Meditation is the basis on which I have built my directed (intentional) intuitive, psychic and mediumistic skillset and it is the basis of how I teach my students. Similar to my childhood camp meditation, I have been able to bring these tools back to my family because everyone can benefit from attaining a peaceful state. My mum didn't find as much relief from my hold and release meditation when I was ten, but these days she uses my meditation tracks daily.

I start every class I teach with a meditation because without meditation, there is no focus. Without focus, you cannot access information on demand. Through meditation, I have learned to access psychic information and to connect to the spirit world. I have used meditation to begin my readings almost every single day for the last ten years. My brain, physical body and spirit body are very familiar with what this 'territory' feels like. I know when I am in a space to be 'connected' and when I'm not. At this point, it's like driving home. When I drive the same road every single day, multiple times a day, I know exactly where I am going. All of my psychic and mediumistic work for clients is on demand, or directed. I tune in to the signal through intention and not as a random experience. Tuning in on demand, whether it is for the intuition, psychic ability or spirit communication, starts with meditation.

HOW MEDITATION WORKS

Meditative states can be studied through brainwaves. The electroencephalograph (EEG), which monitors the brain's electrical activity, was created because of a psychic premonition. The creator of the EEG, a German doctor named Hans Berger, was in the military in 1892 when he had an accident in which he fell off his horse into the path of a gun carriage that almost crushed him.

When he returned to his barracks, his father sent him a telegram checking to see if he was all right. This was odd because Berger's father had never sent him a telegram before. When asked why he had sent the telegram, his father replied that his sister had had a terrible premonition and had asked to send a telegram immediately. This uncanny metaphysical experience was monumental for Berger, who became determined to find a psychic connection between the mind and the outside world. In the process, he created what has evolved to be EEG, which records electrical signals in the brain.

I imagine it would be a joy to Berger to know that EEGs are being used long after his death to study meditative and spiritual states. EEGs have generated some fascinating insight into the brain; they have helped us see that meditation causes real changes in the brain. We now know that meditation changes our brains' waves from beta waves to alpha, theta and gamma waves. At times, when a meditator is in a deep trance state, gamma brainwaves show up.

Brainwaves on an EEG look exactly like that – waves. The faster the waves are moving, the more active your mind is. The higher the frequency of your brainwaves, the more active, alert, and even agitated you are. When your brainwaves have a lower frequency, you relax. Beta brainwaves have a high frequency, and are often the normal, conscious state. As you sit to meditate and your body relaxes, you enter the alpha state, in which you feel like you are not thinking as much alongside a calm awareness. Regular meditation increases the relaxed alpha waves and reduces the more active beta waves. Once in meditation, theta waves emerge, and these brainwaves are characterised by deep relaxation, hypnosis and mental imagery. At times, when a meditator is in a deep trance state, gamma brainwaves show up. In one study, scientist C. Maxwell Cade hooked up spiritual teachers (from a great variety of religious backgrounds) to an EEG and found that they all had the same brainwave profile regardless of their religion. When they had moments of spiritual insight, they exhibited the same alpha, theta and gamma wave frequencies. Perhaps most importantly, Cade documented that with practice, anyone can access these states through meditation (see the Reading and Resources section). He concluded that it is a simple matter of deepening the mind's awareness.

Yes, anyone can learn to meditate and the brain you have can access spiritual states. Meditation is simply any process that achieves a clear mental and emotional state. It is instrumental for learning how to tune in to your intuition, psychic skills, or ability to connect with the spirit world on demand because it slows down the thinking brain.

When the rational mind is very actively engaged, nothing else can come to the surface. As discussed in Chapter 2, the rational mind can be unintentionally disengaged through repetitive tasks. This has a scientific backing – scientists have observed that the same theta brainwaves that are formed in meditation are also predominant in any automatic task: driving, folding clothes, or showering. While these repetitive tasks allow theta waves, and therefore intuition, to emerge, the key to directed intuition (accessing intuition about a topic on demand) is to create an intentionally disengaged mind through meditation.

THE MANY WAYS TO MEDITATE

For those who are new to the practice, meditation often seems like a complicated concept because they focus too much on doing it *right*. Many of my students have told me they cannot meditate, citing that they have too many thoughts. This is a misconception about meditation because it is not possible to turn off all thoughts and it is not the goal. Thoughts are normal and meditation is not about stopping them; it is a practice of watching your thoughts and allowing them to release rather than going down the rabbit hole. This rabbit hole is also known as 'the monkey mind', a metaphor for when your thoughts swing from branch to branch. Through watching thoughts in a meditative state you will gain clarity on the patterns they form. In this way, you can learn to distinguish these thoughts originating from the mental mind's gymnastics from your own inner voice.

There are a million ways to meditate, and no one way is better than the others. Meditation methods range from organised meditations such as Vipassana or Transcendental Meditation to a less organised meditation practice of sitting in silence, painting, exercising, chanting or walking.

Meditation can be as simple as breathing. A common practice is breathing in for four counts and breathing out for eight counts. Simply slowing the breath and relaxing the body tangibly alters the state of consciousness. There is a physiological reason for this relaxation – exhalation stimulates the parasympathetic activity that promotes rest and relaxation. By slowing down your exhale your body is instantly put into a more relaxed state.

Meditation can also get pretty odd. In an effort to find the meditations that work best for me, I'll try it all. My experience with one of the weirder forms of meditation, dynamic meditation, took place at the highest point in Rishikesh, India. The city was visible far below us. Earlier, I had spotted a little sign that read, 'Osho meditation 3p.m.' Seeing me eyeing the sign, one of my new friends said, 'The teacher, Baba G, was a gangster, you know. He went to prison, lost his family, lived in the Himalayas as a holy man, and now has been teaching meditation for twenty years. Nobody ever shows up to his class, but he does the meditation every day and if you want to join in, you can.' I was *definitely* taking this class.

I found myself in a tiny, run-down room with a stone floor and blank walls. It honestly felt and looked a bit like a prison cell.

As the clock struck 3p.m., it became very clear that I was to be Baba G's only student. He was barely 5'1" and looked to be in his sixties. He was muscular, hardened, and had penetrating eyes. 'Former gangster' rang true despite his tiny frame. He silently handed me a pamphlet on Osho Dynamic Meditation, pushed play on an ancient-looking cassette player, closed his eyes, and didn't open them again for the next hour and a half.

It quickly became clear that dynamic meditation was unlike anything I'd ever done before. It was weird. We moved, we flailed, he screamed. Bewildered, I opened my eyes to cheat a look at Baba G, who never once got distracted and didn't give two hoots about what I was or wasn't doing. I could have left and he wouldn't have known. He was fully focused inward.

I finally was able to do the same, and I came into a deep sense of peace, shocked when the recording clicked to a halt. Baba G's eyes opened and he gave me a namaste bow, and exited.

I stood there for a little longer, contemplating what had just happened. I wanted to denounce it as weird, but inside, I knew it had offered me peace. I now know dynamic meditation works through embodiment and movement. It is a meditation that consists of five stages: ten minutes of intense breathing, ten minutes of free movement and sound, ten minutes of jumping, fifteen minutes of stillness and, lastly, fifteen minutes of free dance.

As I descended back into the village, I contemplated Baba G's commitment to his meditation practice. Baba G showed up for his own sense of peace. On a mountaintop in a weird prison-like room. Every day. Students or no students. He didn't look the part, and I'm sure he could have found plenty of excuses not to go that day.

I believe that for every kind of person in the world, there is a meditation that will work for them. Try them all until you find the one you like. Make it weird, or don't. Meditation is for everyone, but there is no 'right' way; the only requirement is to show up.

Quieting the mind, no matter the method, attunes you to your own spirit body. If the outcome is a moment of mental observation and inner peace, then you did it right. If the outcome was simply that you did it, then you also did it right. It is called a meditation practice for a reason: you have to practice it.

PRAYER AND ALLOWING

Some people prefer prayer to meditation, a different road to the same destination. Prayer, like meditation, can also release your rational mind and make room for your intuition. When you energetically enter a conversation within yourself, or with a larger concept of love or God, you open up a space within where inner guidance, direction and understanding can enter.

Shortly after my time with Baba G, I spent some time in an ashram. Ashrams in India serve to provide a place to practise devotional living without the distractions of modern life. I quickly learned that it was *serious*. I meditated, ate, meditated, worked, meditated, sang devotional songs, and finished the night with – you guessed it – more meditation. Everyone had a job, and I was assigned to trash pick-up. If you stayed for a long time, you got a nicer job. It meant you'd braved the mosquitos and the heat and had committed to owning no more than two outfits (that is, material things). I never stayed long enough to be granted a fancier job than trash pick-up, but Claire did.

Claire had been at the ashram for a few years. I first met her when I wandered into the gift shop where she worked, attracted by little elephant necklaces I saw from the window.

As I held one in my hands. I really wanted it. It was of the deity Ganesha, with his cute elephant head, carrying a lotus flower. I've always liked elephants, and Ganesha kept popping up along my travels. I'd grown particularly fond of this deity, known as the remover of obstacles, and I spent some time holding the necklace and putting it back down, weighing if it was going to fit my strict travel budget. As I was busy deciding, I heard a voice behind me say, 'Be careful how you use that.'

This warning came from the sweetest Australian woman. She seemed to be in her early sixties, with straight, loose, white-blond hair down to her shoulders, dressed in a white tunic with a name tag that read, 'How can I help? My name is Claire.'

Glancing back down at the little silver necklace with its smiling elephant, I asked, 'Why am I being careful?' Claire gave a little chuckle and said, 'That elephant's the reason I'm in India. I wanted to be here, so I'm glad he removed the obstacle, but it certainly wasn't how I anticipated this journey.'

Over chai, Claire told me that five years earlier, she had started meditating when she felt incredibly stuck in her life. She got into mantras, read every book, and particularly resonated with the elephant-headed deity Ganesha. As Ganesha was supposed to remove obstacles, Claire decided that day that she would pray, 'Remove the obstacles to my spiritual growth.' As she finished her last rendition of her silent prayer for spiritual growth, an intuitive thought bubbled into her mind to leave her husband. It wasn't a thought she wanted to hear, so she dismissed it, and in that moment, Claire's husband of twenty years burst through the door. 'I have to talk to you,' he said. 'I'm leaving.' He had met another woman some time earlier, but had felt an overwhelming urge to tell Claire in that exact moment.

Claire packed her bags, sold most of her belongings, and found her way to the south of India.

ALTERNATIVE WAYS TO A PASSIVE STATE

I get terrible stage fright. Doing large theatre shows for hundreds of people where I give readings, with no script and no prior plan, was never something I thought I would do. That fear has never fully gone away, so on the day of a show, praying feels like bargaining and passively meditating by counting my breath feels to be effective for only a short while.

While I may find a minute of calm through these practices, I often quickly jump right back into anxiety. I have learned to put some time aside for creative activities like painting and playing an instrument instead. I know that if I do this the day of a show, even if it is hours before the moment I set foot on stage, I will be more focused and able to receive with more clarity and flow.

Meditation works but it is not the only way to get into the desired state of mind. If you find yourself frustrated by meditation or prayer, consider taking out a pencil and drawing pad, dance in your living room, or play an instrument. It doesn't matter if it is terrible artwork, if you can't keep a beat, or if your singing is totally off key – the point is not to be a brilliant artist, but to transition yourself into a creative state.

The intuition thrives when you are activating the right brain, the creative brain. When we get too focused on the patterns, methods and ways to receive we can lose the flow. The intuition is always a right-brain activity and anything that invokes your right brain will also open you up to receive intuitive insights in a more effortless manner.

PASSIVE VERSUS ACTIVE MEDITATION

Each meditation style I have introduced to you at this point is a form of meditation I call 'passive meditation'.

Passive meditation is meditation that aims to bring mental stillness. It is the kind of meditation in which you silence the mind without having a goal of receiving information with intention or direction. Most people meditate in this way, without a desire to access their spiritual gifts or find intuitive, psychic or mediumistic insights.

Passive meditation is a moment of surrender, so while intuitive information is not actively sought, these moments of mental stillness can be enough to allow the information to enter the mind. In a similar way, sleeping can also be useful, as it stops the repetition of worry and anxiety to make room for something else. While passive, it can make way for incredible insight.

There is also a more deliberate way to access the intuition. 'Active meditation' is meditation that aims to actively point your focus in a certain direction and deliberately invite in the intuition you're looking for. This method starts by setting an intention on what you wish to receive, is followed by a passive meditation, and then asks a direct question to allow the information your spirit body contains to bubble up to the surface. You can think of active meditation as taking a metal detector to the beach, looking for the information. In passive meditation, you're just basking in the sun.

You can't get to the active meditation without going through the passive meditation first. Passive meditation is a crucial starting point because when you are 'searching' for intuitive information, it is always easier to look for it from a place of peace than from a place of agitation.

The first step to active meditation is easy: just ask. To move your passive meditation to an active one, complete the passive meditation of your choice until you feel like you have reached a place of mental quiet. From within the quiet moment, focus the insight by asking your spirit body or inner self, 'What do you think?' You can state this as an open-ended question or make it specific to a situation.

The key is to stay in the passive state while you activate the focused question within yourself. For this reason, when you are first starting, my suggestion is to keep it general. Specificity will often get you back into the internal state of the issue rather than the receiving state of the answer. Maintain your passive state and observe the feelings, visions and thoughts that arise. It really can be that simple because your intuition likes to be invited.

INTENTION-SETTING IN ACTIVE MEDITATION

I bought the little Ganesha necklace in India. As a spoiler alert, I didn't lose a husband I didn't have. I also didn't meet one. Actually, nothing particularly earth-shattering happened while I was wearing my necklace. Yet, I did remove an obstacle while I was there, and it was my understanding of how intuitive, psychic and spirit communication work.

My obstacles at age twenty-two were some big questions about my work that kept me up at night. In particular, the overwhelming questions were, *'Is this real?'* and, *'How do I strengthen it?'*

While I was already working full time as a psychic medium, how it worked was still completely mysterious to me.

I was frustrated that in those early years, unlike anything else in my life, putting more effort in didn't always seem to make the work better. When I activated my rational brain to analyse the information, it all disappeared. If I got emotionally and mentally involved, it always got worse, not better. It all seemed counterintuitive; I couldn't seem to make a better connection just because I scrunched my forehead and tried harder.

I wanted some intuitive insight and figured I might as well ask Ganesha to offer me some answers, ideally as quickly as he got rid of cheating husbands. On the very last day in the ashram, I settled myself down on a pillow and set my intention: *'Show me how being a psychic medium works.'*

After a while of sitting and counting my breaths, I entered into a deep passive meditation. When I noticed I had reached a moment of true surrender, I began an active meditation by asking, *'Show me how being a psychic medium works.'*

Suddenly, where before I saw the black nothingness of the backs of my eyelids, I now saw a water fountain in my mind's eye. This fountain didn't have water gushing up; instead, it seemed a little blocked. It still produced a constant stream of water, but it was a small stream of water.

Then, very simply, a thought crossed my mind. 'You are the fountain. For the water to flow, the fountain must be clear. Meditation and prayer makes a clear channel.' With that, the fountain gushed forth water.

That was it. The image faded.

My active meditation emphasised the importance of a receptive mind. If we are a fountain for information (water) to flow through, our fountain must be built well and clear of any obstacles. The way to clear the fountain is through passive meditation.

My own meditation has shifted throughout the years. If I hit a point in a reading where I am trying to scrunch my forehead and think harder, I immediately stop. I take a moment to recognise the current emotional and mental state I am in and I utilise the meditation technique that I know works to shift me out of that particular state. I know the right meditations for my many states through practice. At the end of this chapter, you will find a mix of meditations listed so you can try them yourself.

YOUR DICTIONARY

When I am asked, 'What is the most important thing I can do to strengthen my spiritual gifts?' my answer is always 'meditate, and live a dynamic life in which you collect many life experiences.'

I emphasise meditation because I have experienced time and time again that allowing is more important than controlling in the process of sharpening insight. Your ability to allow is directly proportional to your ability to meditate.

You don't really have to worry about the information, it will always be there waiting to be invited. Instead, focus on the vessel and get it clean and flowing easily.

The second cornerstone of strengthening your spiritual gifts is life experience. When you are in an active meditation, the energy (information) that was absorbed through your spirit body has to be *translated* to the physical body and rational mind.

Your ability to translate the information correctly is in direct proportion to the size of your inner dictionary. In an active meditation, the information can present itself to you through a thought, an image or a feeling. Your method of receiving this information will be different from mine, or anyone else's, simply because you have lived a different life than anyone else has. Your reference points are different and your life experiences have given you a different dictionary than the one I have.

The translating process is one in which your brain does the best job it can to translate the energy you receive into a word, an image, a feeling or a knowing. How you translate will be unique to you and, with practice and continued life experience, your dictionary will naturally increase in size and ability to translate correctly.

I prefer that my students do not look up any symbols they receive. Those symbols are not universal as they were translated to you through your own dictionary. Instead, when a student sees for example a colour in an active meditation, say the colour blue, I encourage them to write down the first ten things that come to mind about the colour blue. Researching what the colour means for the world is not helpful in this case. The information didn't go through the world's dictionary, it went through yours. As the energy hit your spirit body you matched the colour blue as the best translation of that energy you could find in the moment. You didn't cross-reference against the internet and so the answer won't be found on the internet either.

Life experience increases the reference points in your dictionary. The more experiences, the better. There is no end in sight! You will forever be adding to this knowledge base.

ACTIVE MEDITATION FOR EMOTIONALLY CHARGED TOPICS

If you try active meditation for the first time on a stressful subject and ask, 'Are they deceiving me?' or 'Will this business deal make me go bankrupt?', it won't work. While the desire to receive intuitive information about these topics is very real, they hold too much emotional charge. If you are not practised in maintaining a passive meditation state while you activate the question, your mind and emotions will instantly roar to life. Practising active meditation on inconsequential insights and less emotionally charged topics will in time give you the muscle to be intuitive about heavier topics. With time and practice you can use active meditation to intuitively look at anything, no matter how seemingly inconsequential or small.

Years ago, I lived next door to a crazy neighbour who was renting out her home to fifteen people at a time, while she slept in the shed. At least once a week, these people would mistake my house for hers and insist that I was in the wrong place. It was like living next door to a hostel. The landlord couldn't kick her out, so I needed to move right away.

I needed a great spot, quickly, and I found it. While I was really hopeful that it was the right fit, I wanted to check with my deeper knowing, my intuition.

This was an emotionally charged topic for me because I was desperate to move. Therefore, it would not have been effective if I jumped right in and asked for intuitive insight without a meditation process. My mental mind would have been heavily involved.

Before setting my intention I had to complete an extra step. I made an inventory of my current beliefs, worries, fears and emotions surrounding my quest for a new home. I wrote down my longing for a place. I noted my excitement in finding an apartment that ticked everything on my list. I also recognised my anxiety that I wouldn't find something else if I gave up this spot. I noted my fears: that I wouldn't be approved. I also wrote down my desired outcome: that I would find a long-term home.

In an active meditation, writing down your thoughts, emotions and desired outcome ahead of time is important. At the end of your active meditation, if you find that the intuitive information looks exactly like your preliminary thoughts, holds the same emotions and has the exact outcome then it probably isn't the intuition.

After writing down all my initial thoughts, I started my active meditation by setting the intention: 'I desire intuitive insight if the apartment in Playa Del Rey will be a peaceful, nurturing home for me.' My next step was to enter a passive meditation and I chose a gentle breathing meditation.

Twenty minutes in, when I'd attained a state of surrender, I turned the meditation active. I asked my spirit body, 'What do you think?' The intention was already set, so I did not need to be specific.

A solid, peaceful feeling entered my gut. It wasn't emotional, but it was accompanied by a sudden thought that I would move out within a year. I abruptly opened up my eyes and thought, *What?!* I didn't want to move again within a year. It didn't make any sense, especially because I was signing a lease for one year.

I dismissed the second part of my meditation and I focused on the part I liked, that the new spot felt solid and good. I signed the paperwork and moved in. I loved the place and it was a great home, but within seven months a rat infestation came out of nowhere and required me to evacuate. My intuition had been right: within one year, I had to move again. Although it was annoying, it was a good lesson for me to recommit myself to trusting my inner knowing.

When a topic holds great emotional charge, be gentle with yourself. To contemplate an issue while not holding on to a past emotional reaction or expectation of that issue is the goal of even the most advanced Buddhist monks and the meaning of equanimity. This is why often people find it easier to read for others than to read for themselves.

In theory, with a quiet mind and an understanding of your own patterns, absolutely all information about anyone or anything is available to you. The key to an effective active meditation practice is to recognise what is truly intuitive and what is not by comparing your preliminary thoughts and emotions to what arose in the meditation. If they are the same, you were not in a proper active-meditation state. Even if the outcome is the desired outcome, the intuitive information will present itself differently.

Give it a few tries on different days; there will be days when a mindful, quiet mind is easier to attain than others. Similarly, there will be days when intuitive information bubbles up to the surface with ease and days that are more difficult. Being intuitive is less about receiving and more about allowing. Remember that your spirit body holds the information before you know the information. The process of receiving is allowing it to bubble up to the surface. Patience and timing is everything in this practice.

This active meditation practice is the starting point of attuning yourself at will to the information you're looking for. In more advanced practices, the focus can be turned to any person, place or thing in order to 'find out more' or see if it aligns with what you're hoping to create.

This process to accessing directed intuition is not about control, but rather about choice and allowing. You are choosing to silence your mental mind, you are choosing to orient your focus and attention, and you are allowing some space for the information to enter your spirit body, move through your senses, and then enter your thinking mind. If the directed intuition is the act of turning your head towards your spirit body's knowledge, then meditation is the neck that allows this movement to happen.

DO IT YOURSELF

Passive meditations

Try out a new passive meditation technique. I encourage my students to try a new meditation style once a week; they can then choose to incorporate it into their normal meditation routine if the new style works for them. Below are a few meditation techniques to try, but there are many more out there in the world. You can research each one to gain a better understanding.

1. *Square/Box Breathing* – A rhythmic breathing style in which you inhale through your nose for a slow count of 4, hold the breath for 4 counts, exhale through the mouth for 4 counts and finally pause for 4 counts before repeating.
2. *Zen Meditation* – Sit upright and follow the breath, particularly the way it moves in and out of the belly, letting your mind 'just be'.
3. *Mantra/TM Meditation* – A mantra is a syllable, word or phrase that is repeated during meditation. Mantras can be spoken, chanted, whispered or repeated in the mind.
4. *Guided Meditation* – A meditation teacher will guide you through your practice. There are thousands of guided meditations available online and you can find them on my website, too.
5. *Progressive Muscle Relaxation Meditation* – Progressive muscle relaxation is a relaxation technique that reduces

stress and anxiety in your body by having you slowly tense and then relax each muscle.

6. *Loving-Kindness Meditation* – In this meditation, you will direct positive energy and compassion first to yourself and then to others, which helps you let go of unhappy feelings you may be experiencing.

7. *Walking Meditation* – This involves deliberately thinking about how you walk. Feel the way your foot lifts, how you plant it down, and how your body moves.

8. *2-to-1 Breathing* – Exhale for double the count (twice the duration) of your inhalation.

Active meditation

Practise the art of active meditation to gain intuitive understanding about an issue in your life. Choose a passive meditation from the list above before moving into an active meditation. Establishing confidence in your passive meditation first is important because it will help you to shift your brainwaves. You must shift into a receptive mode before entering an active meditation because the mindset and energy of the problem is never the same mindset and energy of the solution.

1. Mindfully think about how the situation makes you think and feel. Write down your desired outcomes and the charged emotions that come up for you surrounding this question. In short, what do you *want* the answer to be? What emotions do you feel surrounding the topic? Where in your body do they exist?

2. Put these notes aside and take some distance. Perhaps go do something else before starting the passive meditation if it's all a bit too strongly charged.

3. Begin a passive meditation that works for you. I recommend it to be at least twenty minutes.

4. Move into an active meditation by, in a state of peaceful reflection, asking the question, 'Spirit body (intuition, inner wisdom, higher self . . . pick the words you like best), what do you think?'

5. Simply notice the response. What do you feel, see, hear?

PSYCHIC ABILITY

———

CHAPTER 5

Psychic Skills

Ten years ago, my friend Liz was one of the very few who knew I was working on my psychic skills. One morning I woke up to a text that her aunt was in the hospital and in a coma. She asked for my psychic help because she and her family needed to travel to see her aunt in Florida, and they had no idea what to expect upon their arrival at the ICU.

I was hesitant to get involved. I'd never really done any psychic work with importance attached to it. I told her not to expect too much, but that I would try.

I knew what Liz felt like, I knew her signal. Through an active meditation, my first step was to psychically find and tune in to that signal. Then within Liz's spirit body, I was able to find the signal belonging to her aunt. This signal would hold the information I was looking for. I followed it to her aunt and the only thing I felt was that her aunt had a lot of pain in her lung. Specifically, her left lung. She would be fine, but her spirit body was showing me that her left lung hurt and it seemed there were teeth in her lungs.

I texted this information back to Liz, and her mum and the family were sceptical. Upon further examination, it had become clear that her aunt had fallen into a coma due to neglected diabetes, so lung issues simply made no sense. However, after further testing, they learned that when Liz's aunt fell into the coma she had swallowed her dentures, which had lodged in her left lung.

This was a moment that was incredibly important for me. For one, I was still struggling with the realness of my psychic ability at this early time in my work. I couldn't rationalise this away because there was no rational link between a diabetic coma and lung pain. Secondly, it indicated that readings could be done from anywhere. There was absolutely no issue with my reading from a distance. I know now that psychic work does not operate within the confines of space and time; if you know the signal of what you're looking for, you can find it anywhere.

Psychic ability differs from the intuition because it is information about other people versus information about the self. Psychic information holds no influence or importance for the person receiving it. When receiving psychic information, to access it, rather than point your attention and focus to the self, you point this focus outside of yourself.

PSYCHIC READINGS

A psychic reader is an ambassador to your own knowing. A psychic reader is someone who tunes in to your signal and then reads what is found in your spirit body. In theory, everything you have ever done or can possibly do is found in your spirit body;

the past, present, and your potential future paths. Psychics can also tune in to the signal of locations, pets, or the patterns of the world at large. You do not need to be a psychic reader to tune in to this psychic information, but a psychic reader has learned how to access the information at will.

We seek out psychics because human life is filled with emotional charge and hardship that can cloud our own vision and block our inner clarity. You could, theoretically, access everything a psychic can tell you through your own intuition. However, in questions that hold great emotional charge, personal bias towards what you desire the outcome or answer to be is hard to get around, and that's why having a third party involved can offer valuable insight.

I think the best psychic readings are a reflection back to the person about things they know to be true but don't trust. A psychic reader is not pulling information out of thin air when they are speaking about your life, they are attuned to your spirit body, which contains the information about you. When you are in great alignment with your own spirit body, the knowledge should not be entirely out of left field.

To begin a psychic reading, I tune myself to the signal of the spirit body of a person or place I am reading. To do this, I enter an active meditation and then place my focus on the person's spirit body and find their unique signal pattern; I tune in to their radio station. The first step in developing the psychic skillset is to differentiate the various signals people carry. The signal is always your point of entry. Before you can attune yourself to a signal, you have to be able to identify and find it. A person with great skill will find that everything is contained within the spirit body and its corresponding signal. Your current life choices, potentials, the past, and who you are at the deepest core of your being.

Anyone can develop a psychic ability, to some degree. The use of this ability is not limited to working as a psychic medium. You can be psychic in any profession, in any field and benefit from it. You will naturally be most psychic about the things you care about; this operates similarly to the intuition in that your psychic awareness is pointed at what you find important.

Many students over the years have expressed real fear of their psychic insight because it never seems to give them happy news. These students know if there will be a plane crash, an earthquake, and one student even had a vision of planes crashing into the World Trade Center the day before the 9/11 terrorist attack. They don't understand why they only receive negative information. The answer is that their psyche is pointed in that direction, consciously or subconsciously. I find that these students are frightened of the world and hold deep fears around dying. In an effort to recalibrate them, I tell them to stop watching the news for a period of time and actively look instead for good things in the world and positive news.

Initially, psychic information can feel and look similar to intuition, but with a closer look will indicate a different pattern. Similarly to the work you did in Chapter 2 to identify how your intuition speaks to you in patterns, you can do the same for any psychic information you have received. By looking back at your past, you will notice that you receive psychic information in a different way than you receive intuitive information. It is important to learn the difference, because you want to be able to proactively know what to do with the information and you can only do this if you know where it is directed.

PSYCHICS IN EVERY PROFESSION

I've witnessed incredible psychic feats I wouldn't believe to be real if I hadn't personally lived them. Master Zhou, an eighty-year-old chi gong master, looked right at a friend of mine and told her she had a brain tumour. Lucy is in her early thirties and had absolutely no symptoms. She wasn't even seeing him for an appointment on that day, she was just tagging along with a friend. After her encounter with Master Zhou, she decided to get a CT scan just to make sure, making up symptoms so the doctor would give her one. Lo and behold, Lucy did have a brain tumour, and caught it early enough to make a full recovery.

My amazing acupuncturist Amy Fleetman in Los Angeles took a look at me after I got ten vaccines in preparation for a trip to India. She explained that she could energetically see the angles of the needles as they had entered my arms, saying, 'How weird. The angles of how the vaccines were administered are different on each of your arms. Generally, doctors go in at the same angle every time. Did the doctor switch hands or something?' I had been to a husband-and-wife clinic; while I sat between them, the husband gave me five vaccines in my right arm and the wife did the other five in my left arm. Two different people were holding the needles, meaning the shots entered my arms at different angles.

A random homeless man in India asked to see my hand and read my palm, correctly telling me that I came from a family of four people, would live in countries I wasn't born in, and would ultimately be a known teacher.

There is a misconception that extraordinary psychic gifts are reserved for a select few or that it is difficult to find the people who possess these gifts. I disagree. Psychic ability exists within every profession. Psychic gifts are everywhere, and everyone has them to a certain degree. I think they'd be even more widespread if we accepted their existence in early childhood and made an effort to understand how they can be expanded upon.

The perceived strangeness of being psychic and a conflicted history of great external judgement towards psychics (and mediums) have often caused the people who enjoy incredible access to their abilities to withdraw from mass attention or to be quite secretive about their experiences. They hide because people who are sensitive to energy will often be sensitive to critique, too. I'm sure you have encountered many psychic people without knowing it.

THE REASON YOU AREN'T PSYCHIC RIGHT NOW

If you don't believe you have an ounce of psychic insight, then there is no hope for you. I say this teasingly, but also with full confidence that the main reason you aren't open to your psychic gifts is your limiting belief that you don't have them. I held incredible scepticism when I first started this work, yet I quickly realised I wasn't going to get very far if I doubted absolutely every part of my experience. Doubting yourself at every twist and turn is like taking two steps forward and three steps back.

Doubt puts the brakes on your experience. Psychic skills can't unfold if you don't allow them to.

We exist within the realm of our own possibility. A limiting belief is something you believe to be true that limits you in some way. This can be about you, others or the world at large. If you accept this limiting belief, that is your truth.

Your beliefs surrounding your own intuition, ability to be psychic and ability to communicate with the spirit world have been accumulating throughout your entire life. They are unique to your life experience and are influenced by others. These beliefs can be, 'I am not psychic', 'Being psychic is not a natural ability' or 'Psychic skills are dangerous'. They can also limit what you believe to be possible about being psychic: perhaps you believe it is possible to read other people's emotions, but it is not possible to read the future. It is likely that your limiting beliefs were formed long ago and have never been questioned.

The easiest way to open yourself up to the potential of your psychic abilities is to figure out what you inherently believe about psychic awareness right now and which of these beliefs could be limiting your current experiences. This will give you a clear picture of the level of openness you are starting from. In the journal entry at the end of this chapter I will invite you to write down these beliefs and then state the opposite of each belief. Pushing against the limits of your belief systems will blast open the doors to your intuitive, psychic and mediumistic potential.

There is a certain openness and self-trust required to develop this ability. Initially, when I held great doubt, I made a promise to myself. I decided that for six months, I would suspend my disbelief. I would stop analysing every part of my experience to allow it to unfold. After six months, I could return to my experiences and pick them apart as much as I wanted. This was the breathing room I needed, a path forward without tearing myself down every step of the way. It is also helpful to remember that you are learning a new language, and in learning that language there will be times when you mistranslate. If you get something wrong, do not sink into a state of despair. Being wrong does not mean you are not psychic; you just mistranslated the information and can learn from this to translate it more accurately next time you encounter the same energy.

You are living within a matrix of energetic information in which everything is interconnected. The idea that we are separated from the energy around us is laughable when viewed through the eyes of a psychic medium. On the contrary: we're swimming in it.

Tuning in to psychic awareness can initially present a lot of internal dialogue that is shrouded in doubt, second-guessing and frustration. For this reason, it can be helpful to bring in psychic tools to help you uncover the information that your spirit body knows but your rational mind is having trouble accessing. Tools can act as a bridge to interpretation and understanding.

READING WITH TOOLS: A GOOD PLACE TO START

At nineteen, after years of resisting, I finally started accepting my abilities and proceeded to buy every book on the subject I could get my hands on. The writers had authority over their gifts, and I wanted that, too. I wanted to be able to choose when I turned myself 'on' to do a reading, and I wanted to choose when I turned myself 'off'.

My desire was to direct psychic awareness, receiving information about other people at will, but I would have to practise. This left me in a bind; it seemed morally wrong to do this to strangers, and I had no one I could practise on. Additionally, I wasn't willing to announce this activity to the world to get willing volunteers; it felt way too vulnerable.

In the books, I found an exercise I could do without telling anyone: psychometry, which sounded like a magic term from *Harry Potter*. The books explained that psychometry was the ability to read information about someone living through the objects they wore or touched regularly – a ring, a jacket, even just a handkerchief carried for a few days. Everything about this sounded very unrealistically magical.

I decided to try it anyway. What really sold me was that by reading objects, I wouldn't have to tell anyone I was psychic, and I could start my psychic practice in secret. I needed an accomplice, so I enlisted my mum for help. For the next few weeks, she sent me packages of small envelopes with one small object in each. She just told the owners she knew a psychic without naming me. Each item belonged to a person unknown to me. As I held each item in my hand, I wrote down what I saw, felt and heard.

It was very simple information at first. When I held these objects, I would see pictures like a daydream or feel pain in my body. I recall one envelope that just had a a single bobby pin in it. As I held it, I saw a dog who was very dear to the person. I saw this person with pain all over their body, and I felt they shouldn't eat fruit to reduce the pain. I was hesitant and embarrassed to share these psychic impressions because they didn't seem very impressive.

My mum insisted I see it through, and to check my work, she relayed the information to the owner of the object. The next day she called me and excitedly said, 'You were right! The person has severe rheumatoid arthritis, fruit worsens their symptoms and pain, and yes! They have a dog.'

Receiving this initial positive feedback gave me confidence. It made me believe something was happening. This secret exchange between my mum and me worked perfectly; that is, until people got too excited about what they were hearing and wanted to know who this psychic friend was so they could book an appointment.

I've since come to understand psychometry as the process of reading the signal, the personal radio station, of the person the object belongs to. Objects collect energetic information and hold it like a memory. When you find the signal of a person held within an object you can read it in one of two ways: by reading the memory, or by following the signal back to the person no matter where they are in the physical or spirit world.

The process of psychometry begins much like the active meditation you learned about in Chapter 4. Instead of focusing on your own signal, you set your intention to reading the object and shift your focus and attention to the object you're holding. With practice, you'll realise every object holds a slightly different vibrational quality, in the same way that every person has a slightly different signal. When I am directing my attention to an object, I am actively looking for the information while in an active meditation state. It often feels like I am holding a string and pulling it towards me until I find what is at the end. Anyone can look for information in this way when they've mastered passive and active meditation.

There are always exceptions, but as a general rule, objects worn with increased frequency will collect a greater density of information, and the signal strength will dissipate with time. Not all objects are going to hold a ton of exciting information, and this will be disappointing to some people. I encountered this when I auditioned with a TV production company. I wasn't told the angle before going into the casting audition, so I was surprised to walk into a room with three very old-looking objects: a hammer, a hoe and a giant wheel. The casting director told me these objects belonged to a haunted house, and they were hoping for a storyline surrounding murder weapons. I touched them and said, 'Sorry to disappoint, but they're just farm tools, regularly used for farming, and they are pretty old, so they don't hold much information at all.' It was not the answer they wanted, but not all objects are going to have a dramatic story attached to them.

TAROT CARDS

The media portrays psychics with bangles, a crystal ball, the occasional black cat and the tarot deck. For this reason, I was highly suspicious of and against tarot cards for the longest time, but I've come to believe that they are actually a useful tool in intuitive and psychic work. I also believe that card readers can be just as 'good' as psychics who don't use them.

Tarot is a great way to start tapping into your psychic (or intuitive) abilities, as it gives the mind something to do. The cards act as another method to disengage the rational mind to access the information your spirit body has collected. Tarot cards pull information out of you and up to the surface, acting as a catalyst to receiving the information. The cards will activate your own dictionary, the one you naturally possess due to your own experiences.

Your spirit body and internal dictionary will work alongside you by pulling your attention to aspects of the card in answer to your question. This question can be about yourself (intuition) or done for someone else (psychic). When you look at one of the tarot cards your eyes may become fixated on the colour red, and then pulled towards the image of the solitary man. For you, red means anger and the image gives you a feeling of sadness. The conclusion *you* draw from this card, based on your own experiences, may be 'this is a man who is angry to be left behind, he feels abandoned'. Someone else may look at this and think, 'red is power and he is setting out on an exciting new journey all by himself!' Your spirit body will pull you to the cards and the images that match the energy of what you are meant to be translating. This translation happens based on your experiences, your dictionary.

For this reason, if you're new to tarot cards, I would recommend throwing away the little book with all the explanations. It's perfectly fine to use tools as a way to jump into your awareness as long as you realise they are enhancing your natural ability, they are not the reason you can access psychic information. Then, truly believe the skill is always within you; it is much more about the interpretation than which card is used.

Any other kind of tool works in the same way. Runes, crystal balls or pendulums are all tools to access the information your spirit body already knows. I believe all tools are secondary to the natural psychic ability you have residing within you, but they can help to bring it to the surface of your awareness. Psychic tools are never doing the reading; you are.

YOUR SPIRIT CORE

In a psychic reading, I read the outer layers of someone's spirit body first. I call these identifiers, the facts of a person's life. Identifiers are what you did, who you did it with, what you're doing, how you're doing it, and where that's headed. The identifiers in a reading sound like 'You've got three kids, you recently had surgery, you are purchasing a new home.'

In a psychic reading sometimes this is all someone is ready for, but the layers of your spirit body go a lot deeper if you are prepared to hear it. The core of your spirit body, your spirit core, is the most true part of your being and it is not interested in whether you are buying a new house. This part of you aligns with your growth, expansion, purpose and life meaning.

I may be an optimist, but I truly believe the spirit core is divine. When I dig deep enough, all people, even those who have made the worst choices, have a pure core. I've worked with murderers, a man who committed major fraud, and abusers. Their actions are not right, but I believe that at their core, they are still inherently good.

Sitting with someone and verbalising who they truly are will often trigger a deep emotional response for the person receiving the reading. When I work to uncover a layer of who you are and reflect that back at you, you get to see the truth of who you are and what you are capable of. This can be a beautiful experience, especially for someone whose life choices have strayed very far from their spirit core. When they recognise their truth, their emotions can be overwhelming.

I once read for a man who came in stubbornly and solely at the insistence of his wife. He sat on my couch with arms crossed, unyielding about all of the information I shared with him. No matter what I shared with this high-powered businessman, he barely made a sound to confirm or reject the information. At a certain point, I ignored him completely and just read without asking for a yes or no. I really thought we'd gotten absolutely nowhere, and as he left my office, I shook it off, telling myself, 'You can't help them all.' You can imagine my surprise when he came back for another reading a year later.

He shared with me that after our session, he'd sat in the car park for half an hour without moving, trying and failing to rationalise the reading away. His whole world had been turned upside down by our session; everything he believed to be true about his physical existence had been shattered. He said he walked around his office in a catatonic state for weeks, unable to work. When he recovered, he changed the parts of his life that he felt were incongruent with the true nature of his being.

Some people are ready to hear their own truths and can shift their lives to be in unity with their true beings, but others are not ready to hear it. Stuart was one of these people. He was a multi-millionaire manager and lawyer. I'd read for his wife and daughter a few times, but I had never read for him. One day he emailed me, saying he urgently needed to see me, and a few days later he sat in my office.

As I started the reading, I saw an impending huge federal lawsuit. He was being sued for a tax fraud scheme. 'Yes, yes,' he said, 'that's happening, but how do I get out of it?' I took a moment to gather my ground before saying, 'Stuart, do you see that you're in fact guilty of these charges? Because, to be honest, it looks like you're guilty.'

'Absolutely not,' was his answer. He wouldn't budge on it, so I told him that regardless of his belief around guilty or not guilty, there was no way he wasn't going to prison. No amount of budging the energy or looking for alternative ways led me to a different outcome. Not long after, I saw on the news that he pleaded guilty and did two years in prison.

His wife and daughter found the recording later and listened to it, amazed that he'd decided to lie and deny even to the psychic he was consulting. I don't judge his experience; we all expand at a different rate. His moment of truth may happen in prison, or it may not. However, as a psychic, it can be painful to see someone dismiss their own truths and, in doing so, disconnect from their divinity. I see that when we are in constant conflict with the goodness of our true nature, our lives are never truly peaceful, even though our physical lives may appear powerful.

The essence of your spirit core is infinite. Your spirit core is the spark of divinity within you that tells you no matter what, you are going to be okay. Your spirit core is that yearning, that desire within you to do more, to be more, to have more, and to share more from a place of love rather than from power or obligation. As cheesy as it sounds, the source is love. Anything that is not coming from a place of love is not in alignment with your spirit core, the trueness of your being.

DO IT YOURSELF

Limiting beliefs

1. What do you believe to be true about what psychic ability is and what can be achieved?

2. Reflect back on these beliefs and identify any belief systems that may be holding you back from gaining access to your psychic abilities, or that may be limiting their expansion. Reflect on the belief system you grew up in, the beliefs your parents held, and how they have influenced your current thoughts.

3. Write each limiting belief out as a sentence (e.g. 'I believe that psychics are born, not made.').

4. Write the opposite of each limiting belief so that it becomes an empowering statement (e.g. 'I was naturally born psychic. I can learn to attune myself to my psychic abilities.').

5. Post a few of these affirmations around your home where you will see them often, such as your bathroom mirror, on your fridge, etc.

Psychic tools

In both psychometry and tarot readings, write down what you receive during the readings. Often, the information will not make sense right away. You can learn to build trust by reflecting back at a later time and noticing what you interpreted correctly.

Psychometry

1. Enter a passive meditation first, and then shift into an active meditation by setting the intention that you would like to read the signal connected to an object.
2. Hold the object (ideally you would not know who it belongs to).
3. Notice any sensation in your body; no feeling is too small. Do you feel happier or more sad than your starting point? Is it a lightness or a heaviness? Do you see any images in your mind's eye? Do thoughts cross your mind?

Tarot cards

1. Enter a passive meditation first, and then shift into an active meditation by setting the intention that you would like to gain psychic information about a person or an event.
2. A simple starting point is to pick three cards.
3. Staying in your meditative state, carefully examine the cards. How do they make you feel?
4. Are there sensations or feelings that arise in your body? Are you drawn to certain images in the cards or colours? What stands out? Are there any thoughts that cross your mind as you look at the cards?

CHAPTER 6

Predicting and Creating the Future

Erik, a particularly well-groomed man in his mid thirties, sat on my office couch and enthusiastically told me about the first time we met, five years ago at a Halloween party, when apparently, I 'predicted' his entire life.

I recalled the party, a night on which for the first and last time I had donned stereotypical gypsy psychic garb including big hoop earrings and positioned myself in the fancy Hollywood mansion's laundry room. I did reading after reading for people in Halloween costumes and word spread quickly. With one time slot left for the night, it was Spiderman's turn.

Erik wanted to talk about the reading he had received that Halloween. He recounted that I had said with full confidence that in the future he was sober and would open up many sober living houses. 'I thought that was crazy!' he exclaimed, 'but now, a few years later, I run a few sober living houses just like you said. I need to know – would that have happened if I didn't meet you? Or, was it always destined to be?'

PREDICTIONS

I have 'predicted' many future events. My favourites are baby predictions and I have received many cute emails containing pictures of these foreseen babies. On one retreat I led, I told a woman she would have a third child and it would be a daughter. She laughed: 'No way! I am done!' Two years later I bumped into her in the grocery shop, and she had a little baby girl in a buggy. It made us both laugh.

I have also predicted not-so-nice things, such as deaths, divorces and financial losses. I now ask before I start a reading if there is anything my clients do not want to know. I did not know to do this in my first year of practising my psychic skills, and learned the hard way. I did an off-the-cuff reading for my friend Isa, who was dating a new guy and was madly in love. She wanted me to read him. I was young and inexperienced so I bluntly said, 'I think you'll date him for exactly three years and then it will be over.' She looked up at me in shock and said she didn't want to know that. She didn't speak to me for exactly three years, at which point she wrote to tell me that they had broken up. This was a lesson for me; I now ask people if they truly want to know everything before I start a reading.

Most people do want to know what is going to happen in the future. They come asking about the future of relationships, finances and health. I think for many people who seek out readings, they go because they want reassurance or direction about the direction their lives are going.

Unfortunately, no psychic can tell you exactly what is going to happen because the future is not set in stone.

I realise that by saying 'no psychic can predict the future' I seem to contradict the many times I have 'predicted' the future correctly.

I have come to the conclusion that the future is both predictable and changeable at the same time. The future is predictable because the vast majority of it is created subconsciously and human beings are creatures of energetic habit. The future can change because human beings have choice. Through choice you can identify your subconscious creations and alter the corresponding trajectory.

You are constantly creating your future. This means I *can* have an influence as a psychic on people like Erik and Isa, but I can also show them how their future can be altered and offer them insight into possibilities they may not be aware of. I don't like the term 'predictions' because I am not reading what 'will happen' as if it is an unmoving fate. Instead, I am reading the life events you are currently creating.

When I start a reading, I always remind people that the future is not scripted. I am looking at the probabilities of what is currently being created and what is currently available for you to create successfully. While some future events are already set in motion, you can often change these events if you can bring conscious awareness to how you are creating your future.

THE CURRENT

In order for anything to happen in your life, you have to be an energetic match to it. Long before an event or person shows up in your physical life, it shows up in your spirit body. You have probably heard this concept described as the 'law of attraction' and that law holds true. However, which events and people you attract into your life isn't about the thoughts you are thinking. It goes much deeper than that.

When I look at someone's future, I see that they have an energetic current that is pushing them to a future destination containing people, places and things. This current of energy and intention is created by an infinite number of (often subconscious) choices that look like blueprint lines.

You have so many blueprint lines! These lines are the beliefs you hold, traumas, hopes, desires, or any kind of pattern that shapes your worldview and experience. They are influenced by dynamics related to loyalty, values and safety. Every single day, you are drawing and redrawing blueprint lines that are setting your current and selecting the direction you are headed.

Without exception, these lines show me that everyone is a creature of habit. Not only through our actions; our energy has habits too. At times, these currents run so deep that people don't realise what they are doing until it is pointed out to them.

When these lines are drawn every day, over and over again, some of them become very thick; a path well travelled. These are the lines that matter. They are the strong emotional beliefs, unchanging habits, repetitive behaviours, perspectives and opinions that you have held for years.

All of these blueprint lines are creating a strong current and direction that gives me, a psychic, the probabilities of your future destination. This is why your future can be predicted. There are generally a few variations to the outcomes, but any psychic prediction is a reflection of the probability of each outcome.

There is great power in knowing what you are currently creating and how you are creating it. You want your blueprint lines to be well defined if they are moving you towards your desired destination, but when they are sending you the wrong way it is time to look underneath the surface.

Our futures are not set in stone, but if we carry on the way we live without taking a look beneath the surface, they may as well be. Most of the world operates this way, and it is what makes psychic predictions possible. While you can be the master of your fate and the captain of your soul, you are doing it subconsciously and you've been setting a course for a long time. The future is not set because it is preplanned, but rather because you've been drawing those same lines for so long that they have formed deep grooves and it is very unlikely you'll change them. Like everyone else, you are a creature of habit. While the future is in a constant state of creation, you fall into currents that don't deviate and they are headed in a direction that is also unlikely to deviate. At any given point, you can choose to draw a new line and go in a new direction, but you probably won't unless you do some digging into why you hold certain beliefs or behavioural patterns.

BECOMING AN ENERGETIC MATCH

I met one of my best friends, Brian, when we were both single and dating in Los Angeles. We lived on the same street and I really enjoyed our almost daily check-ins, especially the ones about our dating lives. At least once a week we would find ourselves on the couch, a glass of wine in hand, discussing our date and current takeaways. When Brian showed me a photo of Steve I was excited for him, but after a few dates Brian told me that he didn't think Steve was interested. There just wasn't a spark.

This was surprising; on paper they were perfect. Brian and Steve are both kind, attractive men and they both waited a long time for someone special. They knew what they wanted – both men are in their fifties and they both wanted a stable and loving partnership. Looking back, while they said there was no 'spark' I imagine neither had a solid rational reason for not being very interested the first time around, other than a feeling or the absence of one.

They went their separate ways and didn't speak for three years. Then they reconnected online and this time, things were really different. They almost instantly fell into a very serious relationship.

Their experience demonstrates the need to be in energetic alignment with a person or experience for anything to move forward. If you aren't ready, you could literally meet a life partner and experience no connection. Brian and Steve had been on dates and got to know each other, but before they were in energetic alignment there was no force drawing them together.

In order for them to be a match they each had to shift energetically.

In their time apart, I saw Brian go to therapy for the first time and really sit down with himself to unravel what he wanted in a relationship and the beliefs he held that were holding him in opposition. He started therapy in June and in December he reconnected with Steve. I believe this was an opportunity for Brian to come into greater alignment with who he truly is and thereby become able to be a match for the kind of partnership he had been looking for the entire time. They each had to shift internally before they could come together externally.

I don't believe their three years apart mattered. What mattered was the deconstruction of the energy currents that were keeping them apart. Before you can find alignment into the future you desire, you have to get clear on what it is that you are currently creating and how you are creating it. It is hard to create from a place of internal conflict and it is impossible to create from a place of misalignment.

Often when I am asked to look at someone's energy to see the possibility of a new partner, new job, or other life shift, the person I am reading for thinks that the power of that outcome is defined by the external world. This is backwards. Attracting anything new into your life is an internal process first and an external process second. To the great annoyance of many people who have visited my office asking about a soulmate, you cannot attract something you are not a match with. When you are a vibrational match, you meet the match. The future shifts when you shift internally.

Many people go through their lives enacting the unresolved pain and drama they carry. The currents based on childhood trauma, familial issues, losses, education, social conditioning and a myriad of other events that we all experience in our lives often continue to play out underneath the surface through and in relationships, work and daily life. All of those currents are subconscious and they are drawing blueprint lines daily.

This doesn't mean you cannot shift them. Once you know what currents you are setting for yourself, you can shift existing blueprint lines that are not serving you and set new ones to create the life you desire.

STAGNATION

The reasons for a person's energetic incongruence with their desired future are highly varied. Everyone is different, but the outcome is the same. The dynamic of misalignment can be most easily spotted in an area of your life where you are not going anywhere, or where things are continually going wrong no matter how hard you push. I have sat in front of a lot of people experiencing this stagnation, because let's face it, no one comes to see a psychic medium when life is going totally great.

One thing I know for sure from sitting in front of thousands of people, assessing their deepest struggles and frustrations: more effort and more screaming isn't going to make the change happen faster.

If there is a place in your life where you find yourself in a stalemate, seemingly not moving forward no matter the amount of hard work and effort you've put into it, then you know you are in misalignment. The areas of misalignment will often appear to me in a psychic reading as a stalemate. It feels to me as if a third of you is pulling to the left, a third is pulling to the right and the remaining third is pulling straight ahead. The result is you aren't going very far very fast. When I see this misalignment in someone's spirit body and bring it to their attention, they always respond with a version of 'Yeah, I just feel so stuck.'

Misalignment doesn't just happen, it's usually the consequence of living life entirely from the subconscious current of learned beliefs, social expectations, traumas, fears and conditioning. At some point, you stopped listening to yourself and instead got swayed by someone else's needs and wants, society's thoughts on how you should live, and belief systems that aren't organically yours. We take on belief systems of inadequacy, low worth, inability. We hold tight to martyrdom and being selfless. We are conditioned to ask everyone around us for their opinion except for ourselves, polling girlfriends and even googling really big life decision questions such as, 'Should I quit my job?' (Genuinely, these queries are googled incessantly.) Misalignment is clearly present when people give internet strangers more credit than their own inner voice. This external search has a compounding effect. Over the years, your own knowing and your own voice get increasingly less airtime.

A CONSCIOUS SHIFT

When I met Valerie, I instantly liked her. She is in her early forties, with big kind eyes and dark hair that falls to her shoulders. She greeted me with an upbeat, perky personality. But while her appearance was fun and lively, her energy told a story of confusion and grief.

I began the reading by taking a look at her present life, which felt nice. I saw a relationship with a partner who looked kind and committed. I also saw that Valerie was frustrated because she wanted to get married but that her boyfriend had not asked. She immediately jumped on this, and practically lifted herself off of her chair: 'That's what I want to know!' *When will he ask? Why is it not happening?*

But her energy wouldn't let me go to the future. Every time I tried to look, her spirit body instead pulled me back to her past, specifically to her mid-thirties. I zero-ed in on age thirty-six. In my body I felt disorientation, as if her entire life had flipped upside down about six years ago. I saw a death, a change of residence and deep grief. 'Am I right to say that you were married before and lost your first husband in your mid-thirties around thirty-six?' I asked her, and she replied that I was.

Valerie's energy to create her future was split in two directions. It was as if she had two blueprints in competition and confusion with each other. In one older and more established blueprint, she is strongly holding on to the past hopes, wishes and desires she'd held with her previous husband. In the newer second blueprint, she was attempting to create a future with a current husband. The conflict of competing blueprints was deeply soaked in grief.

On top of this, she was holding a few deep beliefs in opposition to getting engaged again. She had desired to be married to only one man for life and believed that by marrying another man she was letting go of her love for her first husband. She held conflicts in family values and loyalty. Logically, she could out-reason this, but her energetic currents weren't following suit. Until she shifted her own split energy, the proposal could not happen. When I told Valerie my observations, her perky energy went quiet. She told me that it made sense and started to cry.

I always know we've hit on something big when there is a big, unexpected emotional release. I also know that this is why those subconscious blueprint lines were actively creating Valerie's future. In doing the work to get out of our own ways, a very important distinction to how we create is that the only subconscious blueprints that matter are the ones you have a negative emotional connection to. The others are creating positive change to enable you to move in the direction of what you desire! You do not have to change those. Likewise, neutral blueprints can be ignored.

Valerie may have thought that her boyfriend's resistance to marriage was his doing because to her it seemed like he could just ask, but that is not how our realities are created. It wasn't his fault. The energy simply didn't allow him to ask. This was likely translated to him in such a way that he didn't feel like it was the right time, or felt that he wasn't ready.

I assured Valerie that these competing blueprints wouldn't be in competition for ever and told her that eventually her energy would shift naturally; but that she could take some key steps to shifting it more quickly. I encouraged her to seek out a therapist to help her to shift the beliefs and resistance she holds.

I also knew that this session would immediately help her with shifting these blueprints. The act of observing the subconscious changes it – when the subconscious is consciously encountered it cannot return to its original state.

Valerie could now do not just the grieving work on losing her husband, but allow herself to grieve that future as well and say goodbye to it.

Towards the end of our time together, Valerie's deceased husband entered the reading and validated that moving forward did not mean she was letting go of her love for him. She could love him but move forward all the same. From every angle, Valerie was receiving the message that she could create a new life.

With that, the reading shifted and I was able to move into looking at her future, no longer stuck on her past. New currents were being created; a new blueprint was emerging. I knew she would be getting married, because when our energetic currents line up with something, *it has to happen.* When you create subconsciously, you are creating your future entirely through your programming (beliefs, fears, traumas, habits, etc.). When the subconscious becomes conscious, you run the show.

CONSCIOUS CREATING AND WILLPOWER

Where does that leave good old-fashioned hard work? Don't misunderstand me, action is important. Valerie has to say 'yes!' to a man when he comes along. You absolutely influence your future in the obvious way of making choices and decisions; these are also blueprint lines and they are drawn consciously. However, those actions won't do anything if your underlying energy current is pointing in a completely different direction. You could push really really hard for something, but if your spirit body is not in alignment with what you want, it won't happen and you will feel like you are pushing a boulder uphill.

In our world, we praise willpower and action, and often any failure is seen as a lack of these two qualities. While willpower is an important part of creating the future, it is not nearly as effective as willpower with energetic alignment. Willpower, at its most effective, is the last building block of anything you create. It is ideally the final push once the energy is all lined up and ready to go; the domino that topples it all.

If all your subconscious currents are pointing in one direction and your willpower is pointing in another, with enough willpower eventually that boat *will* move. You can make things happen with really strong willpower and action. But, it would be much easier and much faster to navigate where you want to go when the current is in your favour. Changing your life through willpower alone is the hard way, and if you are pushing against misalignment with this alone, you'll find yourself at a standstill for a while. It will feel like a stalemate in which you're not moving backwards but you're not moving forwards either. Your energy is flowing in one direction while your willpower and action-based orientation are going in the other. I've seen people get stuck in that space for a long time. Pushing and pulling against themselves.

At times, I look at someone's blueprint and I see that no amount of action would overcome their energetic current. When there are millions of blueprint lines attached to emotion, belief, desire and fear in opposition to the action, the energetic current is an unmatched force for willpower.

Furthermore, a decision or action is unlikely to be sustained without energetic alignment. Your entire blueprint system has to allow the desired reality to be created. We can think of willpower as the engine against a current. The engine cannot go on for ever; it will eventually run out of gas.

To create effectively, first identify how you are creating your blueprint and *then* apply willpower. Willpower alone is no match for a lack of clear direction.

ALIGNMENT AS AN EXTERNAL RESPONSE

It is not necessary to be in total alignment all the time for things to go the way you want, but you do have to be in alignment most of the time. I find that if people can get their currents to align to a preferred outcome 70 per cent of the time, it will happen. If 70 per cent of the time their desires, beliefs, habits and choices are aligned to the desired outcome, this outcome will gain momentum and increase in likelihood every day.

That doesn't mean that if you are currently at 10 per cent you will never get what you desire. The push and pull of not getting there, and the resulting recalibration, is an important part of this process. Not getting what you want gets you clear on what it is you want to be creating in the first place. When moments in your life happen that you don't like, you are naturally given the opportunity to move into alignment with what you do want. Eventually, with enough time and bumping into what you don't want, you will adjust your behaviours, beliefs and ultimately currents to create focused creation. There are two ways to create a future in response to life events: bump into the experiences of what you don't want and course-correct to eventually reach at least 70 per cent, or align right away.

When you go the bumpy way, that percentage increases a little every day. Long before you make a seemingly rash decision to change jobs, leave a partner or move to another country, the desire for that particular change and what it offers you has been brewing. However, immediate and instant alignment can happen. When you have a massive reaction to what is unwanted, that makes you shout out 'Never again!', you can shift dramatically.

Even small choices that changed your life are made from an impulse originating deep within you. I can see it in your spirit body years before you take the action. This impulse brews for a long time before it reaches its tipping point and everyone has a different rate of getting to that final moment. Even the rate of how fast you'll reach the tipping point is set in a pattern you hold in your spirit body. This is how a psychic can predict a timeline. It is all a matter of probability based on how you've been living your life up to this point and what that is setting in motion, at what rate.

ALIGNMENT AS AN INTERNAL SHIFT

You cannot mess up your life. If you are finding energetic alignment based on external response, you will eventually bump yourself to where you desire to be going. There is a second way: make the internal shift first. Identifying the energetic currents you desire and cleaning up what is undesired gets you out of your own way. This allows you to get into alignment without having to bump into an undesired reality.

This is a course-correction from within, rather than through an external reaction. When enough belief, desire and inner direction build up, life changes. It has to. Nothing you encounter is ever outside of your own energetic reality.

At the end of this chapter, you will find an exercise that helps you to identify where you are in misalignment and how to course-correct from the inside. This work can be seen as a form of manifestation.

I have witnessed greater progress in my students when they work to create from a place of emotion rather than from a place of visualisation or thought. The energetic currents that stand in opposition to what you want will always hold feelings of negative emotion. For Valerie, she desired to feel safe, committed and loved in a new partnership. The emotions she was feeling were frustration, disappointment and pain. She can use these emotions as indicators that she holds strong energetic currents and blueprint lines in opposition to what she desires. A strong, negative emotional set point always indicates a deep blueprint line that is in misalignment. The blueprints that are creating positive change are moving in a direction of what you desire! Don't be afraid of every sad emotion you have; if it doesn't hold long-term negative emotional reactions in you, it doesn't hold much negative power.

The gap between what Valerie is feeling and what she wants to be feeling is where the magic lies. She will find that her beliefs around loyalty and honouring pain reside within this gap.

CREATING THE FUTURE

You can either be at the mercy of your undercurrent and end up with the life you are subconsciously creating, or you can clear up your negative beliefs and expectations, focus on your truth, and create the life you want.

If you are creating your future through the negative subconscious currents that we have been discussing, then your future is being created without your own deliberate participation. Almost everyone is living through their subconscious current and this is why, when I do a reading, their future will appear very set, concrete even. Ideally, you want to clean it all up and shift your subconscious currents to positive influences so that that you are creating and allowing what you want to enter your life.

If this feels totally overwhelming, consider finding a therapist or life coach you trust. Even a trusted friend can help you identify some subconscious currents you can let go of.

While knowing *what* causes the subconscious currents can be illuminating for the current emotions you are experiencing, I would recommend that you don't get stuck in the past. Ultimately, it doesn't matter what event caused the current. In an effort to shift these currents, it is necessary to give up the need to know why things happen the way they do. Every experience has a growth opportunity, but we significantly stagnate this growth by getting stuck on the experience itself and reliving it over and over again. You will see much more expansive growth in your life by identifying the present emotions you desire to shift rather than getting stuck on the past event that created them. By letting go of the past, you can move forward into a state of allowance of the future you desire to create.

None of this is a race, because you will never be done. You will never mess it up or lose out on the opportunity to create what it is that you truly want. Part of the beauty of free will is that it is a creative process. Every moment of recalibration is a step forward. As your life advances, you will be inspired to create new experiences and opportunities you had never thought of before. The creation of your life is expansive and never-ending.

DO IT YOURSELF

How do we create new currents? By taking inventory of the current ones pushing you along, often unseen. Intellectual enquiry will get you to a certain point but you cannot rationalise the subconscious current entirely because it is not being created by the rational brain. You can intellectually know that you are worthy of a good partnership but still choose abusive partners. You can intellectually desire a new job but not be in alignment with finding one. In the same way, you can't form a new pattern by just intellectualising it, feeling it is where you want to start.

Rather than looking at currents through the lens of intellect, I find that very active currents are more easily seen when we look at the areas of life we hold negative emotion around and the fears, traumas and beliefs that hold those emotions in place.

To do this, take a brief inventory by completing the following sentences:

The predominant emotion I feel in my romantic life is:

. . . .

The predominant emotion I feel in my business and career life is:

. . . .

The predominant emotion I feel around my finances is:

. . . .

The predominant emotion I feel around my family is:

. . . .

The predominant emotion I feel around my residence is:

. . . .

The predominant emotion I feel around my health is:

. . . .

The predominant emotion I desire in my romantic life is:

. . . .

The predominant emotion I desire in my business and career life is:

. . . .

The predominant emotion I desire around my finances is:

. . . .

The predominant emotion I desire around my family is:

. . . .

The predominant emotion I desire around my residence is:

. . . .

The predominant emotion I desire around my health is:

. . . .

If you need some help, return to the emotion wheel introduced in Chapter 3. The clearer you get on the exact emotion, the more empowered you are to shift it.

The gap between what you currently feel and what you desire to feel is where the work is at. For each gap, identify three beliefs, fears, social expectations, etc., that are keeping you from feeling the way you want to feel. A great place to start is by checking your feelings around self-worth, self-acceptance, feelings of lack, ability, and how those beliefs show up in the emotions you wrote out above.

Next, and most importantly, write out the opposite of these beliefs and work to affirm them to yourself a few times a day. As you do, fully feel the new emotion arise from the core of your being. To achieve this, you can think of a different part of your life that does hold easy access to this emotion and then apply it to the area that doesn't. For example, Valerie would write:

The predominant emotions I feel around my relationship are: frustration, fear, grief. The predominant emotions I desire in my relationship are: satisfaction, relief, ease.

Three sentences that identify the gap:
1. I believe that by marrying a new person I am letting go of the love I hold for my passed husband.
2. I have a social expectation that I should only be married to one person in my life.
3. I am afraid to fully let go of the life I had created with my passed husband.

Three new beliefs:
1. My new belief is that I can be fully capable of creating a new and wonderful life that has been positively shaped and informed by all the experiences of my life. I believe that life has offered me new opportunity. When I say this belief I feel the emotion of satisfaction.
2. I allow myself to release any expectations about what my life should look like and how often I should be

married. My new belief is that I am worthy of many loves in my life. When I say this belief I feel the emotion of relief.

3. I know that my connection to my previous husband will never end even if I let go of our previous life goals and plans. We will always be connected and I can love my new partner and continue to love and grieve my past husband at the same time. When I voice this knowing I hold the emotion of ease.

The key to this practice is to fully feel the new emotion rise from the core of your being. Often we are used to *thinking* the opposite of the old belief instead of *feeling* the opposite of the old belief.

To further change your currents, journal on the following:

1. What are three beliefs you hold or things you do that align with what you desire?
2. What are three ways you sabotage?

CHAPTER 7

Purpose

Being a psychic medium has been the largest force of destiny and purpose in my life. Initially, I didn't want to be a psychic medium and I was extremely angry about it. I spent years wishing, praying, bargaining to be anything else. To my great frustration, it never let me forget that it existed. When I was a little girl, ordinary-looking people were popping out of every corner of my world revealing themselves to be psychic mediums. My nanny was a psychic who told my surprised parents that I was one as well, which helped them understand my conversations with the deceased. Our family had a neighbourhood baker who, upon meeting me, shared that he too had psychic gifts. My mother's doctor also shared that he had abilities. Even a random man stopped me at the beach to tell me I would work as a medium without knowing anything about me.

Actually, each of these people told me this would be my work. For years, I was exasperated by these claims and would immediately dismiss them. I told my little sister that they probably said that to everyone. She rolled her eyes and laughingly responded, 'They never tell me that.'

I didn't want it. I told my parents when they brought it up that I had simply been really imaginative as a child. I kept throwing this knowledge as far from myself as I could, and when I finally thought I had succeeded, I became incredibly ill.

I experienced this illness while in college. My symptoms appeared out of nowhere and no doctor could figure out what was going on. No matter how much I slept, even thirteen-plus hours a day, I didn't have the energy to walk to class. I couldn't seem to recover. I took everything out of my diet that could possibly be causing my issues, and I mean everything. I was in bed by 8p.m. every night. I was nineteen, lived with a strict regimen of food and sleep, and yet things kept getting worse. At one point, I could barely get out of bed, I couldn't think, it felt like my head was exploding, and while it isn't a medical thing to point to, everything in my body just felt 'off'. Only three months prior, I had been an athlete and an A plus student and now, I had to take the next quarter off school. I just couldn't function any more.

Things were so bad that my logical, engineer dad encouraged me to make an appointment with a psychic medium. I found one on Yelp and, as related in the introduction to this book, she told me that if I did not live my purpose as a psychic medium I would possibly die. I was used to people telling me I was a psychic medium at this point and was in the habit of quickly dismissing it. She had identified the illness, however, and as much as I wanted to tell myself she was wrong, her words resonated deep inside my spirit.

Does one call that destiny, purpose, fate? It certainly seems like it and it brings us back to the question: what is free will and what is destiny?

While you do create your life, through the blueprints and currents we discussed in Chapter 6, that is the simple answer. The more expansive answer is that you do not singularly create your life, you create it alongside a larger force: your spirit core and the universe at large. This larger force holds your own inner wisdom and is connected to all non-physical aid. Whatever you believe in (God, spirit guides, angels) it communicates with you through your spirit core.

The spirit core is the part of you connected to your divinity and your purpose. Your blueprint lines can either align with or stand in opposition to this larger purpose. To feel fully in alignment, and to fully create the future you want, any future you want, you must hold an awareness of both. You must be aware of what you are singularly creating in your blueprints *and* be connected to the larger force residing deep within you at the same time.

The effort of creating your future from a spiritually conscious place is the process of aligning your blueprints with your spirit core purpose.

For me, the spirit core purpose of being a psychic medium was non-negotiable. At first, my blueprint lines were not in an easy union with this purpose. My original blueprint currents were born in fear. They were old beliefs around not wanting to be different. They were lines of fear around isolation if I was seen as weird. I worked on them, I healed them. I believe their discord with the spirit core was so severe that it was able to create physical illness. I have since replaced them with blueprint lines of allowance and alignment. In this way, I have found alignment with my purpose of bringing people peace. To my relief, the more I have aligned, the healthier I feel.

I am reminded of this destiny when I don't do a reading for a while. I just feel *off*, in the same way as my little sister describes feeling off when she has gone a while without playing her instrument or engaging with her music. We all have purpose and we must align with it to feel like our true selves.

PURPOSE

Late one night, I got a text from my friend Traci: 'Life question of the month . . . is there something we are meant to be doing with our lives??? I mean you found your calling . . . do we all have one?' Traci is not alone in her questioning; purpose is the number one thing I am asked about in psychic readings. My clients are driven to get a reading to find their purpose and my friends are up late at night thinking about theirs. I don't know anyone who has not at some point in their life been frustrated by the process of finding purpose.

Your incarnation in the world is not haphazard or created without direction. Your life is not a random experience and your purpose is not random either. I believe part of my clients' frustration comes from feeling like purpose has to be one specific thing. This is very limiting because the spirit core doesn't hold only one purpose for you and it doesn't often talk in specifics. Purpose exists in every area of your life but it is rarely a specific task; it is more often thematic.

Let's say you have a purpose to find a manner in which to express your artistic nature. You can do this in many ways. You can make music, be an interior designer, chef, or an artistic mother. The possibilities for expressing the artist are endless.

These are the things I know to be true about purpose:

1. Everyone has a spirit core and it always carries purpose.
2. Purpose is a driving force for the expansion of your life; your willingness to listen expands the possibilities of your purpose.
3. You do not have just one purpose in a lifetime.
4. Purpose supersedes specific areas of your life. It can be expressed through and in many ways. While it can be work-related, it does not have to be.
5. Work-aligned purpose is not more important or significant than purpose aligned with a different area of life.
6. Purpose does not remain constant; it shifts in content and orientation throughout your life.

The source of purpose is the spirit core, your connection to divinity and your connection to all that is. When you are connected, you feel alive from the deepest part of your being. The spirit core is the purest of intention and expansion, and purpose is the path to connecting to this intention and expansion. While your purpose will always be there, the degree to which you align with and step into it is up to you. When you listen, the scope of your purpose increases. It will never give you more than you can handle.

I want to re-emphasise that your spirit core, the deepest places of purpose within you, is not always work-related. We live in a society where purpose is synonymous with work and that can create a lot of frustration and sadness. People miss their purpose call to action when it shows up thematically rather than speaking to them through a specific job. Parenthood in all forms is aligned with purpose. Building community is aligned with purpose. Teaching is aligned with purpose. Creating art is aligned with purpose. These themes can be accomplished in many ways. In these cases, the specific path is less important than the larger scope and direction.

Self-enquiry is also purpose. I have even read for people and seen a current purpose that felt like a 'create your own adventure' challenge. They were being asked to look within to create their lives, rather than look outward to what was expected of them. Often people with this pattern show up frustrated because they have felt no clear direction, but that is exactly the point. They are being called to create direction and witness their own power in the process of it.

LISTENING

Purpose can shift during your lifetime. Even when it seems to have a continuing theme, it will shift in orientation and content. I have seen that the orientation of my purpose has already shifted in my life. There were years of my life in which the process of being a psychic medium was pointed inward. These were years where I had to get quiet and venture within to access my expansion. Now, this purpose points outward in a way that connects me to the external world. In writing this book, my purpose of being a psychic medium is aligned with the public. Everyone experiences internal and external years. These timelines are different for each individual person. It is possible that my purpose of connecting with people through being a psychic medium will not be a lifelong purpose, it could shift later in life. Only time will tell!

At any time, listening to these shifts and creating your life from the spirit core is brave. The internal call usually doesn't follow the status quo and it usually doesn't make logical sense. The spirit core does not spend time looking outwards at what everyone else thinks it should do. It isn't concerned with being cool or popular, or with pleasing others.

It is a quiet voice. It will rise through the spirit body, and into your awareness through an intuitive call to action, if you allow it to. No matter how much conflict you create in yourself, the spirit core is unmoving. To create from your spirit core, you have to be willing to listen. I find that once you've heard it, there really is no going back. It is powerful and it is a power you can claim at any point.

I encountered a new call from my spirit core in February 2019, in a dog park. Out of nowhere, I realised it was time to leave Los Angeles.

This knowing came upon me quietly at first, and then all of a sudden. It stopped me dead in my tracks; it was incessant. I volleyed back at my mind that this was impractical; moving internationally is too big. I looked around at the familiar land-scape. I had lived in Los Angeles for thirteen years, it felt safe. I really hoped inner me just needed new furniture or something.

She did not, and the voice kept coming over and over again. I tried to drown it out. I asked everyone else's opinion to convince myself it was all foolish and tried to nest by buying pillows for the house. No matter how much I resisted, it became increasingly apparent that my spirit core had unapologetically pointed the way. The only thing holding it all back was my own stubborn willpower.

My spirit core knew that for my expansion of the self in that moment, I needed new environments, new interactions, connections to different places and different people. This was a purpose aligned to inner self. A purpose aligned to self-enquiry. A purpose aligned with discovery. And the way to move me there was a move across the world.

If you have been confronted with a spirit core call to action, there is no escaping it. I've often told clients who are resisting an inner call that will surely dismantle their lives, 'You can make the change yourself, or it is going to be made for you.' The thing is, your spirit core will give you a few chances and maybe even a few years to get on board, but it isn't going to stop calling.

When people get fired, lose relationships or have financial losses there is always a spirit core call, from long before, that went ignored. If you are honest, you already knew you weren't in the right place. Your spirit core will only wait so long. Just as I had told my clients, when I didn't listen my life became increasingly more difficult. Everything that could go wrong did go wrong, and I began to feel super stuck, more stuck than I had ever felt before.

After almost a year of resisting, my world exploded. The choice was made for me. Within two months' time, I was without a house in Los Angeles during the beginnings of a pandemic. No home, no furniture, no relationship, no office and no in-person clients. Save for my dog, a car and too many clothes, it was all untethered.

Initially, I searched for Los Angeles homes and was completely uninspired because I knew I didn't want to live there any more. This call, the one I had ignored a thousand times, couldn't be ignored any longer. The message was clear: you are not staying in Los Angeles. Go.

It took some time to sort out the pieces but I found myself on a plane and then in a new place. People asked over and over again, 'Why Lisbon?' and I had no idea. I could see everyone's concern; I had never visited Portugal, didn't speak Portuguese, and didn't know a single soul there. I didn't care. I was tired of not following the voice, and my inner knowing told me I would be happy there. The spirit core doesn't speak in outcomes or in how the future will form and that is why most people do not want to follow it when the initial call comes. When you have not yet learned to trust yourself, the call can be scary. Most of us have to be told many times over.

Things flowed easily from the moment I made the decision. Work aligned itself perfectly, even in the pandemic. Two months later, I was on the phone with my mum and she was looking at a promo video I had just captured on camera. 'You've got a sparkle back in your eyes,' she said, 'I haven't seen it in a while.' She was right. I was really happy. If I had had any doubt about making the move, it was gone.

THE 5 PER CENT

I will be honest and tell you very few people create their lives by aligning with their spirit core above all else. Maybe 5 per cent of the people I read for are truly aligned with their spirit core. By doing so they hold the great freedom to creatively shape their blueprints to match their purpose. When I read for these people, I usually want to thank *them* because it is so inspirational. They are truly alive, expansive, vibrating at their maximum potential. They are living from their spirit core.

When people are fully connected to their spirit core in an area of their life, they can move mountains. We look at these people and we see the potential of humanity. It seems as if they have what it takes to be visionaries. Yet it is not only access to this vision, the inspiration, that is important. They must align *all* of their blueprint lines with their spirit core. They have to trust to such a degree that all of their currents, subconscious and conscious, are aligned with this spirit core knowing. That is true power.

I remember hearing an interview with Lady Gaga where she said, 'I've felt famous my whole life.' Take one look at her musical career and you can see that she lives and breathes her art and never second-guessed her ability to succeed, even when the outer world doubted. Someone like Lady Gaga is able to achieve success when they truly align their blueprints and currents with the spirit core. However, she would only have been able to access a vision this large if she held the capacity to nurture and manage her currents, her many blueprint lines, to fully honour and align with the vision.

The other 95 per cent of people I read for create their futures to maintain an illusion of being safe. That doesn't mean that they are cut off from their spirit core. They do hear the pings and messages, but they don't fully trust their spirit core and so the full potential of their vision is never revealed.

The people I see for psychic readings know their spirit core wants them to leave the relationship, move, change jobs, or create. They bump into this knowing repeatedly but they don't want to leave the safety of what they have in exchange for trusting their spirit core. They are therefore constantly playing catch-up. When you live your life in this way, you are responding to life rather than creating it and in turn, you are limited in your ability to create freely.

That's okay, it's human! Even the 5 per cent do this in areas of their life where they hold more resistance. It doesn't mean you have messed up your purpose; everyone gets where they are meant to go eventually and it isn't a race. Sometimes, it just takes some time for you to get yourself and your blueprints on board. Many people have to bump into their purpose a few times before they listen.

Ultimately, what defines the 5 per cent is that they listen to their spirit core before taking the rest of the world into consideration. They know that no one outside of themselves has the one true answer. There are people who have answers, but those answers ultimately have to align back to your spirit core to be of any use to you. Society has not conditioned people to look within and so it is incredibly hard. We have all been taught from a young age that others know best. The 5 per cent know this is a lie. To belong to the 5 per cent you have to trust your own spirit core before looking outward.

CREATING FROM THE SPIRIT CORE

I read for Claudia once a year for three years in a row. Each time I would say, 'I think you desire to leave your husband. I see that he is cheating on you and you are cheating on him. You both know this, but neither of you has vocally admitted it. This wouldn't be an issue, if that is what your spirit core desired. But, you feel very unhappy to me.'

This was far from a surprise to Claudia. She knew she wasn't happy. She had gotten the message from within herself to leave many times, but she just didn't want to hear it. Every year the message was the same and by the third reading, I recognised her.

When you completely ignore the inner call to go, like Claudia did, your first indication is that you become unsettled. That unsettled feeling can be repressed by blueprint currents like 'what will my family think', 'I can't survive on my own' or 'I see no way out'. Claudia could try to convince herself to stay, but her spirit core did not subscribe to these beliefs.

I was relieved when Claudia once again sat down on my couch and I saw in her spirit body that she had left her relationship. Most importantly, it was a great relief to Claudia's spirit core and she told me she couldn't believe it had taken her so long. Once she surrendered, her life offered many opportunities to help her go. With every move forward, people came into her life to help her along and she ultimately married a man she was truly happy with. 'If I had known it would lead me to so much happiness, I would have gone years ago,' she told me.

A spirit core call to action can be a scary knock to answer, because it requires you to dismantle your life without showing you the destination. Rest assured that when you get that call, a new life is waiting for you. I have never, not once, heard someone tell me they regretted a spirit core call to action. No one gets the call if the time isn't right and better things aren't waiting on the other side.

No matter if you are listening or not, the spirit core will keep knocking. You can't escape the core. While initially you have a choice, ultimately life forces your hand or you get too tired of playing it safe. I have seen that when someone truly learns to trust their spirit core, the world looks on in wonder. The magic is, anyone can do it.

There is no good or bad, no right or wrong, there are no shoulds; the spirit core does not speak in those terms. No matter where you find yourself now, the spirit core is accessible to you at all times. It doesn't get more powerful if you listen to it or not, it is powerful by its very existence. The spirit core is not defined by your attention to it. It is always there, ready for when you choose to focus on it.

FRUSTRATION

No one comes to see me when their life is great. They end up in my office stuck or in a state of grief and ask, 'Well, what should I do?'

When people are really stuck, sometimes I get stuck too. I find their signal, read their spirit body and look at their blueprints, to find total chaos. They are at war with themselves and their blueprints are going in all sorts of conflicting directions.

In these moments, I go deeper and turn to the deeper spirit body core.

No matter how much conflict you create in yourself, the spirit core is unmoving. This is true for everyone: Your spirit body core wants you to create and it wants you to expand.

How do you know you have hit a spirit core truth, a spirit core purpose? It is the feeling of being deeply and truly alive. Perhaps creating art gets you there, being with family, creating community, connecting people, healing people, self-enquiry and times of reflection, or loving animals. If it lights you up, it expands your spirit, and it is thereby connected to the spirit core.

Your desires can point you in the right direction of purpose. Desires are often neglected as a transient, silly want. But desires can point the way to your joy, and your joy points the way to your purpose. Often, what lights you up requires a moment of personal risk. It may not be what others think should light you up and it may even appear selfish. Yet the spirit core asks you to be brave and to put your own alignment first, knowing that if you are aligned, your expansion will allow others to expand alongside you.

The first step to finding purpose is making some space to get curious about what you desire without shame or blame. Allow yourself to peek inside and see what is in there without fear of doing it wrong or letting down those close to you. True alignment with the spirit core will never hurt anyone, as it is always the path to a more expansive version of you, which gives others the inspiration to do the same.

This is the divine part of you and this divinity simply does not care if at this moment you've created a real mess, because it knows that in any moment you can shift out of it. It knows you are a being in motion and in constant creation. Even more, it knows that the timing of when you do this is of zero importance and when you are ready, you will shift into a new reality or reality will shift for you. There is never a reason to think that you've wasted time or that it is all too late for you. Time is limitless when it comes to your divinity.

PUTTING IT ALL TOGETHER: THE SHIFT

The people I know who are most successful listen to themselves. They align with their purpose and spirit core connection and then liberally use free will to creatively fill in the details and shape the life they want. You can do this too.

It doesn't mean you have to be enlightened without any old subconscious currents getting in your way. It is likely those will never be fully eradicated. Subconscious currents are part of a human life and you will probably continue to work through them until you cross over. This isn't a process of getting it done, this is a process of listening to your spirit core while becoming aware of your currents through trial and error.

You want to live a life in which every day you do your best to get your spirit core, actions, desires, beliefs, and all other currents acting in unison to create the most expansive version of yourself.

When you do that, you have full autonomy to get as creative as you want on how you wish to fill in the details. Life isn't about getting it right – you can't. You need to bump into things you don't like, in order to create the ones you do like. And when you do hit those challenges, listening to the spirit core will always help you navigate your way back to expansion.

To understand your spirit core and understand the blueprint current shaping your life and how it aligns with your larger purpose and divinity, you need to get quiet. Understanding how you are showing up energetically can initially take a bit of emotional heavy lifting and self-enquiry. At times, that inner truth and that little voice need some time to mature. It is only with compassion, with self-love, that the parts of ourselves that are hurting can be allowed to be heard and our deepest desires can be acknowledged. In softness, we heal and let go of our fight to keep certain energy currents going that aren't helping us live a good and peaceful life. The way to the spirit core is often found in allowing the true inner you a chance to speak, and being gentle with yourself when it doesn't.

Shifting your currents may require major subconscious changes based on your new conscious awareness. Your core beliefs aren't likely to change overnight – but they could. Your fears likely won't disappear in a moment – but they could. Your desires have been shaping themselves for a long time, but they can shift too, or become more focused. Be gentle. It is a process.

DO IT YOURSELF:

Answer the following journal questions:

1. What makes you come alive or gives you joy? If there was nothing standing in your way, no financial or other limitations, what would you choose to do with your life?
2. Where in your life have you felt most connected to your purpose? What do you believe it to be in this moment?

Limiting beliefs

1. List all the activities you completed this past week. Of these activities, pick three that felt nourishing to your spirit.
2. Of these, which ones stand out the most?
3. Make a commitment to implement this activity into your next week and expand on it.
4. Set a day aside this week in which you will notice your desires without question.
5. After, reflect on whether this is a desire you were surprised to find.

SPIRIT COMMUNICATION

CHAPTER 8

The Exit Points of Life

Courtney and her mother, Tina, have visited me once a year for the last six years. Tina's daughter and Courtney's sister, Briana, was only eighteen when she passed from cancer. Briana has come through in every reading I have done for her family. She is always fun, showing up in readings with colourful fingernails, a different colour on each nail, and an artistic flair. Each time Courtney and Tina came to visit, Briana communicated that she was aware of the changes her family had gone through and knew of the many ways in which they continued to honour and celebrate her.

A year after our first reading, Courtney was pregnant for the first time. She wasn't showing yet, but Briana mentioned it right away. At the end of the reading, Courtney said, 'Can you ask my sister and father if they can watch over my baby? Will this baby be okay?'

I said, 'Your sister needs you to know you'll have a little girl that comes into the world. She'll be healthy and wonderful. They are going to make sure she gets here.' Courtney didn't know what the sex of the baby was yet, and she felt that this meant her sister was telling her she was having a girl. It came as a surprise, then, when she found out her baby was a boy.

The next time Courtney and her mother came in for a reading, I turned my attention to the spirit world and found the signal of a new spirit body, a baby boy. Courtney had sadly given birth to a stillborn son. We were able to connect, and the message was the same: a healthy baby girl is coming.

Over a year passed, and the next time I saw Courtney, she was pregnant again. This time, Briana said, 'This is the baby girl who is coming into the world!' I was shown that this little girl would have a prominent red birthmark. A few months later, Courtney did give birth to a healthy baby girl, and she does have a significant birthmark.

I often marvel at the spirit world's intelligence and tact in delivering the news of a passing. Rather than tell Courtney her baby boy would be stillborn, she was told she would give birth to a healthy baby girl. Courtney didn't understand the meaning at that time, and she understandably assumed I had been wrong about the sex of her baby. It is tragically beautiful that in this way her sister was able to communicate that the baby boy wouldn't make it. I do believe there is a certain relief in Courtney knowing she couldn't have changed the outcome, that she did nothing wrong.

I encountered a similar moment of spirit intelligence when I was doing a reading for a woman named Alison, who was in her forties. She wanted a psychic life reading, and she wasn't very impressed with me. For one, I told her that she owned a business with a man she had known for many years, but in the following year, they wouldn't be working together.

'That's clearly wrong,' Alison snapped. 'We've worked together for eighteen years, and the business is booming! We definitely aren't going to stop working together.' She left disappointed.

I didn't see her again until she signed up for a class of mine a year later. After class, she came up to me and shared that her business partner had unexpectedly died of a heart attack at the young age of forty-three. 'Why didn't you tell me he would pass?' she said. 'You knew we wouldn't be working together, but maybe if I knew he had a bad heart I could have prevented it.'

EXIT POINTS

Our cultural ideas about death make it so that we feel we should try to stop it at all costs. I believe this is why death is rarely brought up in a direct way in a reading; it is so that the receiver of the message doesn't feel responsible for having to change it. In cases when the receiver doesn't feel this responsibility, the information is given more literally. In one such case, I told a man his ailing mother with dementia would likely be passing in November. She did pass in November, and the information gave him time to visit her one last time.

I don't decide who gets the direct insight and who doesn't. In the case of Courtney and Alison, I was not privy to this information either. I give what I get.

In readings, I've had people directly ask me when someone will pass. 'Should I fly home this weekend?' has always been a nicer question than, 'When will I get my inheritance?' But, in both instances, what they are asking is, 'Is there a moment? An exit point? A predestined time at which we go?'

There are exit points; however, your spirit body always gets a say. An exit point is a moment during a person's life when their spirit is given a choice to depart from this world. The spirit will consider its exit point prior to the moment of actual departure, and the choice to stay or go is further evaluated at each exit point. Some people have many exit points before they hit the one that takes them to the other side; these people seem to have nine lives, constantly avoiding danger or near-death situations. Others will simply have one exit point. At each exit point, free will is taken into account, as well as the completion of purpose. It's my belief that one can override the other.

Sometimes the experience of deciding not to pass at an exit point is an extreme moment of soul growth for that individual because they touch death in a way that is more intimate than they have yet experienced, as in a near-death experience (NDE). This moment can positively change the trajectory of a life, acting to align someone back with their spirit core.

Although we may not always know when someone will pass, I find that the spirit body of the person passing does. They are always aware at least on a subconscious level, and sometimes the information bubbles up to the surface into their conscious understanding.

THE SPIRIT BODY ALWAYS KNOWS

I received the call while in New York City heading north; the city skyscrapers turned blurry as my vision clouded over with tears. Nathan had died last night. I tried to get to the train, taking the wrong one in the wrong direction, replaying what I had heard, trying to make it seem more or less real.

The security guy took one look at me and didn't even ask for my ticket.

Nathan was my best friend's boyfriend. He and his friend were driving back from an orchestral performance when they swerved to the wrong side of the road. Nathan was completing his master of art in music degree in Boston, and my friend, Sophie, was starting hers in San Francisco. They had met during their undergraduate studies. A week before Nathan's passing, Sophie moved to San Francisco to begin her master's programme.

His passing seemed abrupt and in all ways unpredictable. It was clearly an unintentional accident. However, looking back, his actions had been bizarrely predictive of his passing.

Despite not being home for the summer, Nathan had made a great deal of effort to spend time with his family in the weeks leading up to his passing, uncharacteristically telling them he loved them and patching things up. He also made a number of phone calls to friends, one of whom was an administrator on Sophie's master's programme, without telling her. Nathan had asked this friend to watch out for her and give her some help. Later, this was crucial, as it allowed her to take some time off without having to explain the tragic news because the administration already knew of their connection.

There was also a poetic beauty to Nathan's last moments. Two nights before his passing, his dream, which is every trumpet player's dream, came true and he performed the famous trumpet solo part in Mahler's Symphony No. 5. This trumpet solo opens the piece and it is part of the 'Trauermarsch', which is a funeral march.

Mahler wrote this symphony after surviving a sudden haemorrhage that almost killed him. It is said that in this fifth symphony out of nine, he makes peace with death. Nathan wasn't originally meant to play the principal part on that night, but a last-minute change gave him the opportunity to play the coveted trumpet solo. It was his last major concert.

It is not uncommon for people to tell me that their loved ones experienced foreshadowing events or did uncharacteristic things before an unexpected passing. Calling people to say, 'I love you,' writing cryptic messages on social media, or in one case that was recounted to me, hugging everyone for a particularly long time before walking out and getting into an accident.

I believe the spirit body always knows when it's going to pass. At times, this awareness will rise up into the consciousness to influence actions and behaviours. Similar to the way undirected intuition gets your attention, the person will do or say things that don't make sense in the moment but seem almost predictive when looking back. If you are very connected to your spirit body, you might even know when you are going to pass. The Brazilian medium Chico Xavier famously said that he would die the day that all of Brazil was happy, cheering and clapping. Many eyes were rolled; everyone said *that* day would never come. The day Chico Xavier died was the day Brazil won the World Cup.

HOW WE DIE

Over and over again in a reading, those in spirit will tell me the same things. 'While I was passing, I heard you, I felt your kiss, I knew you were sitting on my right-hand side, I knew you were thinking of me hundreds of miles away, I visited you while you slept, I came to see you even when you didn't know I had passed or I knew you were on your way to the hospital.'

If you have questions about what your loved one sensed as they were passing, rest assured the spirit body is incredibly aware as it transitions. Their ability to be aware of your presence extends far beyond the physical room they occupy. I remember one reading I did for a woman whose friend in the spirit world had been a priest in his lifetime. He showed me he had an awareness during his passing of multiple places at once. Prayers said in the church, the presence of many family members who were actually far away, and a gathering of fellow clergymen around his bedside. While all of these people existed in three separate countries, he was simultaneously aware of all of their thoughts, prayers and actions. When we release the physical body, we also release the limitations of time and space.

In a reading, I frequently receive information about the number of people in the room during the passing, where someone was sitting, the timing of the passing, or what was happening in and around the person. These are always facts given to reassure the family and friends left behind that the spirit body was definitely aware of these last moments.

I've seen in readings that the spirit does get some say in how and when they pass. If they need permission to go, they often wait for their entire family to get there. Other times, they wait until everyone has left their side to pass. As a general rule, this is often because they find it too difficult to let go of the earthly body when the people they want to stay for are in the room.

Although the spirit is aware of everything that is happening, this doesn't mean there is a great awareness of pain. Transitions always feel easy, no matter the circumstances. Additionally, no matter how someone passes, there are always people to greet them on the other side. Family, friends and pets all greet someone as they cross. A question I get asked often is, 'Why do people die in bad ways?' I don't believe there is one answer. Just as the timeline of your life is unique, so are the reasons for your ultimate departure.

HOMICIDE AND FORGIVENESS

When I'm on stage and reading for an audience, I find that my most detailed and strong readings are those connected to tragic passings. Once, after a show, a lady came up to my assistant and said, 'You can tell she really likes the homicides.' When he recounted it to me, it made us both laugh because it sounded incredibly dark.

I don't know if 'like' is the right word, but she's got a point in that my most detailed and powerful readings are generally connected to big, tragic deaths. These deaths leave great ripple effects and a deep need for healing. Those in the physical world do not see the joyous continuation of life on the other side; they are only looking at the physical realities of the death.

It is easier for us to celebrate that 'someone is in a better place' and accept a joyous transition into the spirit world for those who are elderly and have lived a long, beautiful life. It is more difficult to accept a passing when it comes to the harder, sudden deaths. Homicide seems unreasonably tragic from our side of life, and it is. Through the lens of our own grief, it is hard to understand why bad and painful things happen. When I'm walking around in the world, living my normal life, I also don't find it easy to wrap my head around the human tragedies I see. I will admit that the first homicide case I worked on with a detective gave me nightmares. For weeks, when I closed my eyes, I flashed back to the crime-scene photos I had been handed in a big manila folder in police headquarters on a quiet Sunday afternoon. I couldn't close my eyes without seeing the images spread out on a table in front of me. In those moments, it is easy to forget the joyous nature of the spirit world.

Connecting to these images is reading the past physically. It is the residual memories of what happened, and it can be stomach-turning. Yet this information is just information. It happened, like a memory. What brings me comfort is that the physical reality of how someone passes holds no bearing on the joy I feel when I connect to the existence of the spirit body on the other side through spirit communication.

The moment I connect to the victims in the spirit world, everything feels different. No matter how terrible the passing, there is always peace and always an understanding that death was simply a moment in a much larger picture of life expansion. Those in spirit show me that death is a fairly small part of our larger existence. No one can cease to be. Death itself is a process of continued evolution and expansion and serves as a new experience of growth for your spirit body and spirit consciousness.

I have never felt like any spirit person was obsessed by or stuck due to the manner of their death. I also do not feel them to hold resentment or anger towards a person or event that led to their passing.

It doesn't mean that those in spirit don't have a vested interest in what happens to murderers. There is always awareness and participation. A tragic death can offer those in spirit the opportunity to play a role in the purpose of bringing justice to our physical world. I have witnessed those in spirit who passed by homicide to work alongside detectives here in the physical world to prevent similar events from happening. While their involvement can continue, the spirit person always expresses forgiveness to those involved in their passings.

In my podcast, *Moving Beyond*, I work alongside Claire Bidwell Smith, a grief therapist. Our motivation on the podcast was to merge the two ways of healing grief, traditional grief therapy and mediumship, which are often seen to be at opposite ends of the spectrum. In our first season, you can listen in as we work with Erik Jensen, a man who had done twenty-two years in prison for murder.

His story was dramatic. At seventeen, Erik walked in to witness his friend Nate murdering his mother, Julie. He helped to cover it up. They were tried as adults, and Erik was convicted of first-degree murder and sentenced to life in prison for the murder of Nate's mum. While there, he had some major revelations in his own life that led him to start restorative justice programmes for other men in prison for murder.

Erik spoke to Claire about his own grieving process and his ultimate awareness in the journey of forgiveness. He recounted how he had changed his entire life and felt the strong call to give this event meaning. Erik started investing in other people and in community and, for the last ten years of his incarceration, he focused on helping others. In the podcast, Erik tells Claire the hardest part of his grief process was to forgive himself. Initially, he felt like it was a betrayal of Julie to forgive himself. Yet with self-compassion, he was able to move forward.

In her last words with him before his reading with me, Claire asked Erik, 'When you were in solitary confinement, was there ever a time when you tried to talk to Julie?' Erik briefly paused and then said, 'Definitely, I think (murder) is maybe the only thing on earth where you're not capable of getting some kind of forgiveness or restorative justice with your victim. Not that it always happens in other cases, but it ends up that you're having to have that conversation in your own head instead of having that conversation with another person.'

It was my time to do a reading for Erik, and I had no knowledge of why he was there or who he wanted to connect with. Initially, the reading was hard for me. I looked around and found very few people connected to Erik besides his grandmother. All of a sudden, his grandmother indicated to me that Erik had felt responsible for another person's death. Julie entered, and the rest flowed easily.

Julie indicated that Erik had never taken another person's life again, that he had not been personally responsible for her death, and that she forgave him for the role he played. After she solidified her connection to Erik by recounting some of the facts of the case, what was most profound for me was not only the forgiveness Julie presented but her desire to work through Erik for expansion. I told Erik, 'At one point, you're going to speak to large groups, speak to young people . . . (Julie) will be with you every time you do that, she will join you on stage, every time. It feels necessary, and it feels like it will continue. There is power in it, and you are making a difference. There is a platform that you step into over the next ten years that she wants to be a part of, and it gives meaning to her life as well. You're moving into a space in which you have a voice. Every time you step into that space, call forth the power of people who have passed because they are acknowledging you to have a life that is bigger than your own self. You can have the joys of life, all of them, but your platform is bigger than that. You have the power to tap into this because you've worked through the shadow self into a space of clarity. That is something you can use to work with people on a similar trajectory.'

This case was hugely moving for me. Murder is tragic, but all tragedy can be transformed into progress. When a spirit body transitions, they have their expansion. They are free. All spirit people hope that their death also offers the ability for growth to those left behind in the living world. I believe that is what ignites my desire to work so hard and deliberately for the hard deaths. The reconnection changes the trajectory of lives.

SUICIDE, ADDICTION AND HEALING

The preservation of life is important and necessary. By accepting a passing and forgiving it, we are not saying that it couldn't have been altered had everyone in the equation received healing in life. Yet the truth of life is that not everyone heals in this earthly body and in this timeline. For those who do not heal, death is not a failure. Culturally, death is seen as the absolute worst thing that can happen to you. That is not how the spirit world views death.

When healing is not available to someone on the physical side of life, healing always happens on the other side. Death is an opportunity for healing, too.

As spiritual teacher Ram Dass said, 'Death is taking off a tight shoe.' The transition to death, and to the spirit world, is simply inevitable. No matter the manner of passing, how tragic it was, or how hard the fight, death is not a lost battle. Death is a return to love, expansion and joy. It is a transition we will all make. It is joyous. While those left in the world feel the grief, those on the other side know that their separation is only temporary.

When healing does not happen in the physical world, it always happens in the transition. In the case of suicide, the spirit body passes to the other side just like everyone else. There is no in-between state, no one gets trapped or goes anywhere 'bad'. No matter the way someone passes, I don't believe anyone gets stuck, ever. The spirit body is highly intelligent; it doesn't get stuck.

In some instances, suicide is not an act of free will but a consequence of a mental and emotional misalignment with the physical vessel. When someone crosses due to suicide, their death is never seen by the spirit world as that individual's only option in that moment. There were always other paths and options. The desire for a radical release from physical reality can be very real, but whenever I have connected to someone in the spirit world who chose to go through suicide they recognise that there was always a more practical choice.

There is beauty and peace on the other side, but the choice to find it in the physical world is always available. No matter the many options of finding peace in the world, the choice to find peace on the other side instead is always understood by their spirit body. No one is limited in the spirit world because of the way they chose to enter it.

Any kind of death related to addiction is met with similar understanding in the spirit world. These earthly difficulties do not follow anyone in spirit. Once the physical and mental body is released, the spirit body is free of these hardships too.

DEEP GRIEF

Death can feel so final, and grief can feel like immense disempowerment. Difficult deaths, or any death, can cause a feeling of stickiness as if the grief will never lift.

During grief, happiness can feel difficult to reconcile. Perhaps, like many grieving people, when you feel happy you also feel guilty. You shut down these happy moments. You may tell yourself, 'I have no business being happy given the reality of my story and loss.'

The spirit world does not want you to deny yourself happiness. If there is one thing I hear loud and clear from those in spirit, it is that they wish to see you live the best life possible. Those on the other side want you to return to your joy. That is the unconditional love they have to offer.

DO IT YOURSELF

If you have lost someone and feel you didn't get the opportunity for closure:

1. Write a letter to your loved one in spirit and spill out onto the pages everything you would have wanted to say, what you wish they saw or what you wish they heard. Write it all down.

2. Do a passive meditation holding your letter and invite them into your space. Without exception, they will be there. Allow this experience to unfold without doubt of it being real.

3. Afterwards, you may choose to keep the letter or burn it.

If you are moving through deep grief:

1. Choose a day this week to do an activity that brings you simple joy. It can be a walk outside, a living room dance party, painting, preparing your favourite meal, or singing loudly along to the radio.

2. When you begin, invite your loved one in spirit to join in with you for the fun.

CHAPTER 9

Language of the Spirit World

Two men sat on the couch in front of me. Fernando, who spoke fluent English and a little bit of Arabic, and Joey, who spoke fluent Arabic but only a little English. Also part of the reading, but sitting on her own couch 4,000 miles away in her home country of Iraq, was his mother Shela. To make this work, Joey held a phone to his ear that connected us to Shela.

We were all gathered to connect to Shela's deceased husband, Abraham. We needed all these people because Shela did not speak a word of English and I do not speak a word of Arabic.

If this seems like a complicated situation to you, it was. I started the reading in English and spoke to Fernando. Fernando, in turn, translated my English to Joey in half Arabic and half English.

When we were all in agreement about what I wanted to say to Shela, Joey told Shela what I had said in fluent Arabic.

After this literal game of telephone, Shela would listen on the other line, respond 'yes' or 'no', and we would begin again.

It certainly took a long time. With each bit of information, we collectively paused and heard it go down the line of translations and then back again.

All the same, it worked. Abraham was able to properly communicate many details to his beloved wife. He showed me that his wife wore only black, even ten years after his passing. Abraham described building the home she continued to live in with his bare hands, alongside his brother. Abraham spoke of their four children and how he had seen the new grandchildren. In short, we connected. It did not matter that Shela was located in Iraq and I was in California. Nor did it matter that Shela didn't speak English. It didn't even matter that Abraham had also never spoken English in his lifetime.

We needed a team of translators, but Abraham didn't need a team of people on the other side to translate the information to me. The spirit world does not operate in a language, it operates through the energetic body and corresponding signal. All spirit communication is offered spirit body to spirit body; I found the signal, my spirit body communicated with Abraham's spirit body and translated energetic information contained in both to rational thought, and then into English.

The spirit world doesn't have a voice box and it doesn't need language. Spirits communicate through energy and vibrations that hold a great deal of information because the spirit body is composed of an infinite number of separate energetic identifiers. As a metaphor, imagine the spirit body as white light. We know that when white light hits a prism, it creates a rainbow of colours. All white light is composed of many many different vibrations that equal a colour. In this same way, when Abraham's spirit body connected with mine, it contained many individual vibration identifiers that told me who he is or was. Identifiers such as, he has four children, he built a house with his own hands, or he lived in Iraq. All these identifiers exist as a vibration and it is my job to translate them into English.

I do have a voice box and for my work to have any value, I need to translate the vibration my spirit body receives into a language. My spirit body connects to the spirit people on the other side, their energy and vibration, without too much issue, but the process of translating from energy to conscious knowledge is a bit trickier. My body holds a dictionary that over time has learned to match most vibrations to an image, thought, sound or feeling. In short, I see, hear and feel in an effort to translate and match the energy I am encountering. This is not always a conscious process. My physical body, which is the bridge between my spirit body and my brain, will often react to the information by translating it to the best of its capability instantaneously. Similarly to when you hear a spoken language you are familiar with, you are not consciously translating every sound you hear; it forms meaning immediately.

Matching meaning to energy vibration is like hearing the vibration of a music note and knowing it is the note 'A'. When a musician hears this note, they will recognise it. It is a vibration translated into an auditory sound, hitting the listener's ear, and the brain matches the sound to the knowledge, 'That's an A!' If you've never heard an A being played before you might have to go all the way through the keyboard to find the one that matches. In the moment you hear that note and are able to match it with the A on your keyboard, you will know to translate that sound vibration to its verbal meaning.

Learning the language of the spirit world is similar. All energetic information holds a vibration and my conscious brain will match the meaning of it as best it can. In the beginning, when you're not very good at the language, that matching game can be off, and you can mistranslate. But in time, you can hold a conversation.

MATCHING VIBRATION TO ITS CORRESPONDING LANGUAGE

I believe I get a little bit better at translating things correctly every day. I also know I don't always get it right; there are an infinite number of information and combinations possible. Even in moments where I've fully calmed my brain down, there are still times when the communication doesn't go without a hiccup. However, I am comforted by the fact that miscommunications also happen between two living people. Sometimes, a miscommunication can even be the best moment in the reading.

Albert had committed suicide by hanging himself in his study. His wife, Beatrice, was completely distraught by his passing. In fact, tears streamed down her face the minute she sat down on my couch. Albert was a charming and witty man and I greatly enjoyed the hour during which I got to know him. However, about forty minutes into the reading, we hit a snag.

In a daydream-like way, I saw an image of a gold plaque; it seemed to be inscribed. The image evoked a feeling, a feeling of a memory of work along with an upwelling of pride. Immediately following this image, I saw the plaque displayed. The image changed to a plaque in Beatrice's hands alongside the feeling of grief. I knew she had received it for him posthumously.

This is where mediumship can be tricky sometimes.

I turned to Beatrice: 'Would you understand that he received a gold plaque after his passing for his work? It is one that is displayed and you would currently have,' I said, matching the feeling and images of what I had received to the English language in the best possible way.

'Not at all,' she said. 'He didn't do any kind of work that he would have received a plaque for. I didn't receive anything.'

I turned back to Albert, who gave my body the feeling of a push. The translation: keep going. Again, I saw a gold plaque and the emotion I associate with a job or work well done.

'Are you sure? This is very clearly about work of some sort, and it's definitely gold.' But I was met with a shake of the head and a definite no. I moved on with the reading.

A few weeks later, Beatrice's sister-in-law was scheduled for a reading and Beatrice came with her. They couldn't wait to show me what they had brought along. Out of the depths of an over-sized handbag came a small gold plaque. It was round and engraved with the words, 'May The Work I Have Done Speak For Me.'

Beatrice had selected this small plaque after his death to be displayed next to his urn. 'I can't believe I didn't remember this!' she said. It was now clear that Albert had been trying to talk about the work he had done in his lifetime, just not in the way I had literally translated it, as a career achievement.

I used to be very annoyed when there was information in a reading that my recipient didn't understand. Now I know that this is sometimes the best kind of information I could give. I love when information that someone believes to be false is in fact true. It emphasises that the spirit person was present, and often also has the added benefit of moving the reading along to other family members and friends who can verify the information.

PSYCHIC OR MEDIUMSHIP

I have had many people come up to me after a show and say something along the lines of, 'How can we be sure you are connecting with a spirit world? What if you are just reading me psychically?' That is a very good question and one I pondered for many years.

The psychic argument is not far-fetched. When you lose someone, it will absolutely be in your spirit body and therefore is psychic energy that is available to me. Sometimes when I do a reading I can tell who that person has lost before I even turn to the spirit world. I feel that information psychically.

We know your spirit body contains infinite amounts of information; it contains your past, the people you love and have loved, your present and the probabilities of your future. When you lose someone of significance, information about them will be available in your spirit body.

All the same, as a medium I can feel the difference between a psychic connection and a medium connection. When I do a psychic reading, I am connecting to your spirit body contained within a physical body. My attention and focus is oriented towards you. When I do a mediumistic reading, I am connecting to a spirit body without a physical body. It feels different and the interaction feels different, too. Unfortunately, you would have to take my word for it until you could explore and experience it yourself.

To answer the question in a more tangible manner, I turn to additional experiences that have solidified my own belief that there is consciousness and intelligence separate from our own. One of my favourite moments took place during an audience reading in Orange County, California. A sweet grandfather came through to his granddaughter that night. He gave me some great details – how he would brush his little remaining hair over his very bald head, how she had been his primary caretaker, and details about her mother and his other daughters here in the world.

Towards the end of the connection, I clearly saw him eating out of a tin can. The can wasn't fancy. I knew it appeared to be beans mixed with something. And I received the feeling that this was a very regular way he ate his meals.

His granddaughter's confused look told me she had no idea what I was talking about. But I couldn't shake the image and feelings, so as I turned to start a new reading I said, 'Ask your mum, I think she'll know.'

The show ended and my assistant and I went out for a celebratory glass of wine before heading back home. While in the restaurant, I felt a tap on my shoulder and turned around to find a very excited and tearful woman. 'Guess what!' she exclaimed. 'I just got off the phone with my mum and she said that my grandpa worked on the railroads for years. He would heat his food up in a tin can and eat it sitting alongside everyone else.

That's how they ate their daily meals!' The confusion had been resolved.

At that same theatre show, two young boys came forward who had passed in an accident. It was an aunt of the family who was in the audience to receive the message. After many validations, one boy showed me he had owned a green motorbike and the other said his was yellow.

The woman told me she had no idea what colour the motorbikes had been. But she would ask. After we got back from the intermission, she was excited to tell me that she had called her sister-in-law and the colour had been correct! Her nephew's green motorbike was his favourite bike and she showed me a photo of him, with a wide grin on his face, riding this bike. I felt it was a fantastic way for the mother of the boy to feel a part of the reading that night.

When the spirit world knows more than the living, I am amazed. These moments have helped to answer my biggest questions on how the spirit world works. It shows an intelligence in the spirit world, and an intelligence that exists beyond the only people seemingly in the room, me and my client.

WHO THEY ARE NOW

'She's not going to drop it even from the afterlife?' Paige sighed after I somewhat tentatively told her that her deceased mother was fussing over the cleanliness of Paige's home. Her mother was a 'clean freak' who would have guests sit on a plastic cover on the couch. In the reading with her daughter, Paige's mother brought up the fact that by her standards, Paige could do a little better to keep tidy. Paige had heard this over and over again. She walked out of the reading laughing that her mother certainly hadn't changed a bit.

While it is true that her mother communicated her point of view, it wasn't to bug Paige. It was to validate that it was *her* mother and that she was still seeing Paige's home. I truly believe that when we cross, the drama of our lives melts away. Paige's mother doesn't actually care about the state of Paige's house because she knows life is more than that. Yet those in spirit can't show up as pure energetic wisdom because if they did, we would not recognise them.

I am often asked if people change when they cross. The answer is yes, and no. Parts of you remain the same, because the spirit core divine part of you always existed. Other things fall away. The one thing I know for sure is the that the spirit world is not stagnant. You're certainly not stuck being the person you were here; unfortunately you're also not instantly enlightened. It's a continuation. You're going to go on learning at whatever pace you decide.

Here in the world, we are continuously discovering and uncovering new bits of information about who we are. However, our personalities are often simply identifiers. They are not you at your core. You are not your personality; your personality is a creation. When you cross over, your personality doesn't get stuck in the way it was formed and developed within your lifetime.

As conscious beings we grow and we develop, we change and we alter, we find a better version of ourselves day by day, as hopefully we are doing in this physical world right now. However, I think the spirit world knows that we identify with our loved ones through personality and characteristics. They use that knowledge to let us know that we are connecting to the 'right' spirit, the one we want to be connecting with.

If, for example, someone's father abandoned them and never had a nice thing to say, they wouldn't recognise their father if my introduction to him was, 'I have a really lovely gentleman here who is praising your life and loves you very much.' It is likely that my client's initial reaction would be to say, 'That doesn't sound anything like my father. I don't know that man.'

It is the spirit person's job to identify themselves as we would recognise them, meaning sometimes they come in with personality characteristics that were uniquely theirs but may not be who they are now. In order for a spirit person's messages to be conveyed in a way that gets your attention, they have to communicate who they were. In a reading, we have to focus on who someone *was* to convey who they are now.

Let's say your uncle was a tough guy who rode motorcycles and was remembered by his handlebar moustache. When my spirit body interacts with his, the information of his moustache is identified and conveyed to me by a feeling in my body, in this case the feeling of a moustache on my face.

He doesn't have a moustache right now, but it is an identifying part of who he was. If he rode motorcycles, I will feel myself on one. I ride a motorcycle myself, so he will use that experience to give me a brief memory flashback of that feeling.

These are energy identifiers that I have a working vocabulary around and they offer me moments of recognition so that I can summarise his characteristics and tell you, 'I have a man who feels to be your uncle. He has a big bushy moustache and rides a Harley.' There is no missing him if your uncle was in fact a Harley-riding man.

I may then say, 'It feels like your uncle struggled with alcoholism.' This very real feeling of alcoholism can confuse beginner mediums and they may interpret this as if your uncle is still struggling with alcoholism. That is not the case. While your uncle no longer struggles with addiction on the other side, in order to convey his messages of healing he would have to indicate this experience. Even though that identifying energy still exists within his spirit body, it doesn't mean it is an active struggle. In a reading, when I voice previous drug use, alcoholism, depression, or any human condition we see as difficult, it is immediately lifted and I can feel that it is simply a memory. Not a reality.

Language is another example. Abraham no longer needs language, but when we were speaking to his wife, his spirit body still held the vibrational feeling of someone who spoke Arabic and not English. He has no use for that now, he doesn't need either language to speak to me or anyone else in the physical world, but it is part of how we would recognise him.

In this same way, children are not stuck at the age that they passed. All souls are ageless; it is only the physical experience that gives us a timeline. Their connection to you as your child is not dependent on their age. They will always be your child and will also get to experience expanding in the spirit world.

All physical illness is left behind. I recall a reading I did for a woman whose mother had suffered from severe Alzheimer's in life. Towards the end of her life, her disease was so progressed that when her husband would enter the room, she would greet him as her brother, and she was completely unable to recognise her own children. Her daughter wanted to know, did her mother have any memory of the events as they transpired? Had her spirit been present in those moments? While her mother did indicate her confusion during that time, she showed me that she had since been able to revisit every memory without the cloud of mental confusion. Not only was she completely free of her disease, but her spirit was also able to revisit and fully enjoy the many wonderful exchanges of love. Her spirit body had been aware the entire time. While our personalities, likes and dislike, struggles and experiences are a physical memory that was part of a physical life, it doesn't mean the spirit world doesn't have a sense of humour (sometimes considered a personality trait). In contrast, I have found those in the spirit world to be quite funny.

As an example, I was scheduled to do a theatre show the morning of Easter Sunday. The night before, one of my best friends had teasingly asked me, 'Do you think Jesus would ever show up?' I told her not to be silly.

The next morning, as I stood in front of the audience, I began the connection with a father who wished to communicate with his daughter. The reading was normal in all ways. He had three girls, passed of a heart attack, and wanted to let his wife know how much he loved her. As I finished the connection, I said, 'I can't believe this, but would your father happen to be named Jesus?' As it turns out, Jesus was the first to show up that day after all!

STARTING THE PROCESS OF COMMUNICATION

One of my favourite mediums in the world, Tony Stockwell, likes to say, 'You cannot be wrong, you can only misinterpret.' I agree.

When you are first learning a new language, you are going to mix up some words. When you are learning the language of the spirit world, this is also going to happen. Adding to the difficulty, unlike with a spoken language the language of spirit is not set. The language of spirit operates in a manner that is unique to you, because it uses your personal experiences and your own understanding of the world to convey meaning.

To illustrate this, think about your own mother. Then, try to place the emotion that this memory evokes. When I'm doing a reading and this emotion rises up in me, I know I'm speaking to a mother in the spirit world. But, the way I feel 'mother' may not be the way you receive it and it may not be the emotion that arises in you; your relationship with your own mother will be different from the one I have with my own.

Furthermore, mothers come in many forms. For beginner mediums, all mothers are going to feel more or less the same. With time, they can start to feel more nuanced. There are step-mothers, adoptive mothers, aunts, grandmothers who raised you, older sisters who acted as mothers, foster mothers, etc. A beginner medium might see each of those people as simply a mother, not recognising the slight distinctions in vibration contained within the spirit body. In this instance, the beginner would believe themselves disconnected when they have only misinterpreted.

When I first started working as a medium, I felt like the spirit world was putting me through my own crash course.

Every day there was a theme and it was up to me to find it. A particularly memorable day was 'Sweden' day in which my first appointment was a Swedish woman, the second person had lost a man who was from Sweden, the third was planning a vacation to Sweden, and the last was moving to Sweden. This 'theme of the day' exercise continued for years, giving me an opportunity to spot energy patterns repetitively so I could learn them well.

In theory, I believe everything can be communicated if the vocabulary for it exists. It is possible to convey even very detailed information if I have the right words to match the energy I come into contact with. I experienced this in a reading I did for a very well-known deceased screenwriter and director. His daughter, towards the end of the reading, was sceptical. This is common with people who are very famous because so much of their life is available online.

She ended the reading by asking, 'Can I ask you who his favourite composer was?' As I turned to him, I immediately knew the energetic match to be Mahler, a composer I am very familiar with as a musician myself. While this seems like incredibly specific information, it was only available to me because of my own musical knowledge. It is much more difficult to find a match for an energy I have never encountered before.

MATCHING ENERGY

Good mediums can tune to any signal and any identifier and recognise it. I don't think everyone can learn to be a medium who reads for others, because your antenna may not have access to the sensitivity of tuning to every station imaginable.

Yet, everyone can connect to their own loved ones in spirit. You can connect because you already know their radio station. You know it because you experienced their spirit body and their signal in this physical world and so your spirit body already has a point of recognition for it.

The work you are doing when you are tuning to the spirit world is the work of matching energy. You can also do this backwards. By fondly thinking of a person in the spirit world, you are naturally attuning yourself to their spirit body signal. This will allow you to feel their spirit body. In the beginning, this will feel as if you are simply imagining it. Allow yourself to suspend disbelief so you can have the experience.

Matching energy patterns is also the energetic reason people like to hold objects belonging to passed loved ones. Recall from Chapter 5 that objects absorb a spirit body's signal. Feeling the signal in the object can help you bridge and match this signal to those in the spirit world.

Alla came to see me clutching a watch. I felt that it belonged to Alla's father who was in the spirit world. When I said he was in the room, Alla was immediately visibly relieved. Her father was her only family, and he was gone now. 'I've lost the only family I've ever had; I'm so alone,' she told me. Alla, along with her sister Rachel, had inherited her father's house. The sisters had been close before their father passed but now, they weren't on good terms. Alla's father showed me that their greatest point of contention was what to do with the property. He showed me that Rachel was eager to sell the house, but Alla loved spending time there.

Alla was obsessed with the house. Everything she moved she would put back exactly as it had stood, meticulously placing it in the way it had been the last time her father was in the room. Alla's father showed me that his daughter was insistent that nothing was moved, not even an inch.

When I told her this, she responded, 'Yes, I make sure everything is exactly how he left it, because it's the only place I can feel like he's around me.'

Alla's father wished to communicate to her that although he loved her connection to the house, he was around her constantly and certainly not only in his home. He was free to move in and around the world wherever she would go. With practice, she could learn to feel him anywhere if she found the match. Objects may be able to help her bridge the divide initially, but it wasn't the only way.

In matching your energy to those on the spirit side, it is easier to connect with a loved one in spirit on a happy day than on a sad one. They do not exist in a space of sadness, so it will be hard to connect when you think of them in that way because their vibration will not match the vibration of sadness. In the same way that you cannot tune in to a radio signal if you are miles away from it, you cannot tune in to a signal you are not matching.

Recently, I was doing a reading for a woman who had lost her sweet six-year-old boy to cancer. She asked me why, in moments of intense grief, she cannot feel him. However, when she is in a space in which she is calm and peaceful, he is right there. 'Does he not comfort me when I am in grief?'

Of course he is there in moments where her sadness is overwhelming. He shows up right away. It is her own awareness that is tuned to the wrong station. She is not a match for his vibration when she connects with him from a place in which she imagines him as sad and suffering. His spirit body is alive and vibrant. While she is looking for him in grief, he is still there, she just can't feel him in that moment.

People often ask me if my work is sad, but I feel quite the opposite. I get to connect people not only to their loved ones, but to the understanding that their spirit bodies are alive, well, and in a place of true love. Connecting to that expansion and love feels amazing. It does not feel sad at all.

You have a spirit body, so you can communicate. Everyone can. You may never be fluent in the language of mediumship, but you can certainly increase your comprehension levels, simply by paying attention. Whether you can feel them or not, your loved ones are not far away and they are eager to connect and interact with you.

DO IT YOURSELF

Find a spot where you can sit quietly. Begin by fondly thinking of a person in the spirit world. Select someone you know and who would like to work with. Sometimes, this exercise has better results initially if you work with someone who does not invoke deep grief or heartache. That doesn't mean it is impossible to do it with someone you are currently grieving. Once you've tried it with a more neutral person, you can try the exercise with someone whose loss you are currently struggling with.

Remind yourself about their qualities and how it felt to be in their presence. Visualise and feel them placing their arms around you. Open your awareness to their presence and see if you can feel or sense them.

1. Begin by sitting in a passive meditation space.
2. When you feel like you are calm and peaceful, invite your spirit loved one by asking them to step in.
3. Imagine their hands placed on your shoulders, standing right behind you.
4. Ask them to shift their location to your left-hand side and observe what that shift feels like.
5. Ask them to shift their location to your right-hand side and observe what that shift feels like.
6. Ask them to stand where they feel they can most easily connect with you.

CHAPTER 10

Signs

In the modern world, going inward isn't always easy. If you've ever been overwhelmed by grief or sadness, you know that everything can feel very muffled during these times. I often see that when people are overcome by emotion or by life's demands, the spirit body's information can be hard to detect. Those in the spirit world know the pressures of the modern world. When you aren't feeling them around or hearing them, nor seeing them in your mind's eye, they can get your attention externally through signs.

My grandpa Frits didn't believe in an afterlife. Only a short while before his passing, my aunt asked, 'Dad, if you're wrong and there is a heaven, can you give us a sign?' He promised he would.

Frits was witty and stubborn, and I loved him deeply. I was so obsessed with gaining his attention that when we visited, I was always the first grandchild awake. I didn't want to share him, so I would very slowly and quietly make my way down the very narrow, creaky staircase so that none of my cousins would wake up. My little secret was that in the early hours before everyone woke up, I would watch him shave and then we would sit on the floor to play Monopoly. It was just the two of us, while the sun was rising, playing Monopoly.

My grandfather was a headmaster of the tiny school next door to where he lived. It was the smallest of communities – so small that it was not until the late 1980s that the town began using house numbers (the postman didn't need them; he knew where to find everyone). The night of his passing, a perfectly healthy forty-year-old tree fell in his backyard. No one heard it fall. There were no storms or strong winds. It did not hit the house, the car, the other trees, or his carefully planted vegetables. In fact, it narrowly missed everything and caused no damage at all. That in itself was a miracle.

It was weird. This tree was so wide and large that all of his little grandchildren had to link their hands together to surround it. Inexplicably, it was completely uprooted. When they learned that the tree had fallen, people wondered out loud if he had caused it. Not only because it was bizarre, but also because this was *his* tree.

Grandpa Frits was an avid gardener. Many of the memories I have of him include his garden or the smell of dirt. He planted what he ate, and he always turned to the earth rather than the heavens for answers. He had planted this tree in the 1960s, and carefully placed it to the side of his vegetable garden to provide the perfect amount of shade.

Was it a coincidence that my grandfather's tree fell, or was it a sign, a connection to the spirit world? My aunt decided he had kept his promise to her – to send a clear sign that he wasn't too far away.

As a psychic medium, I believe a sign is a path of communication between the spirit world and ourselves. Few of these signs are as large as a tree falling, although it does happen. The ones that are quieter, such as recurring butterfly visits or repeating numbers, require us to participate. They require us to acknowledge their presence and perhaps even to play a helping hand.

THE SPIRIT BODY AND SIGNS

Sahar travelled all the way from Seattle to see me again. It had been six years since our last reading, and truthfully I didn't remember her when I opened my front door, and I had no memory of the reading we had done together. This isn't unusual; I often forget the facts of a reading hours after doing them unless I write them down.

Sahar wanted to connect to the spirit world. When I start a spirit communication reading, I look for the signal. You now know that each person has a signal of their own, and that's where I begin. In this process, I never ask someone who they want to connect with. Instead, these initial moments feel like I'm scanning the radio stations to see what signals appear. Often, there are multiple signals coming from different spirit bodies.

As I sat down to do a reading with Sahar, I took a moment to scan and focused in on one signal. He stood out to me, standing slightly to my right. As my spirit body connected to his, the identifiers within his spirit body were quickly interpreted to give me the feeling of a young man. Additionally, his signal felt familiar. I knew I'd spent some time with him before.

The young man in spirit standing to my right was Sahar's best friend, Brian, who had passed in an accident. He spoke about their friendship, the events going on in Sahar's life at the moment, his family, and many other details.

After the reading, Sahar said, 'You told me six years ago that Brian would send me a sign, a yellow convertible.'

'A yellow convertible?' I questioned, surprised at my former self. I made a quick mental note to try to sound less crazy in the future.

'Yes! And it happened!' Sahar continued enthusiastically. 'About three years after I saw you, his brother John posted a photo of his new car on Facebook. It was a yellow convertible. I freaked out. I don't really keep in touch with his brother, but I had to call him and ask why in the world he bought a yellow convertible.

'John said that when he went to buy a convertible, the car dealer only had the yellow one on the lot. He didn't hesitate and just bought it. It was unlike him, he said, to make such a sudden decision, but it just felt right.'

'I sent John and his mother the recording of our reading. The part where you said, "He will send you a yellow convertible." They were so amazed . . . three years later . . . how did he do that?'

I have a theory, and unfortunately it doesn't include the spirit world creating yellow convertibles out of thin air for everyone. Instead, I believe those in the spirit world can use their spirit body to nudge your spirit body to make decisions.

SPIRIT BODY TO SPIRIT BODY

You know that both John and Brian have spirit bodies. John has a spirit body here in the physical world, and Brian has one in the spirit world. This gives them a commonality, a way to communicate. John isn't a medium, so he probably didn't realise his brother had paid him a visit. His mental mind wasn't taught to pay attention. All the same, when Brian's non-physical spirit touched his brother John's spirit here in the living world, John made a decision based on an internal pull he couldn't explain rationally.

In the moment that John walked onto the dealership lot, Brian's spirit body silently communicated with John's spirit body to 'Buy the car!' Yet, that was not the starting point.

I believe it's highly likely that John woke up that morning with a strong desire to go to a car dealership. John may not have given any rational thought as to why he wanted to go. He simply had a gut feeling, a desire, or even a need.

Brian nudged his brother to go to the car dealer that day, a day when they only had a yellow convertible. John simply experienced this nudge as a desire to go. Once there, John felt a strong pull towards the yellow convertible. A certainty. John would have experienced all of these as fleeting feelings or a feeling of intuition. He likely didn't pay much attention to where any of these feelings originated. Even if he was asked, I think he likely would have said, 'It feels right,' or 'I just know.' Most people don't recognise the moment a spirit body in the spirit world comes into contact with their own spirit body. Instead, they feel an emotion or a pull from within.

As a medium, I feel a lot more than a pull, but the mechanism of communication is the same. Brian's spirit connects to my spirit body in the same way he connected to John's. The only difference is that my radio station is more sharply tuned and fixed to his signal, and my mental mind has been instructed and developed to make room for the information Brian's spirit body holds.

In this case, Brian in the spirit world was able to interact with his brother John in the physical and nudge him towards a yellow convertible. I think it can sometimes take the spirit world years to finally get us to pay attention to a spirit nudge; in this case, it may have taken Brian three years to get John to pay attention instead of dismissing it.

I believe those in the spirit world interact with us whether we are mediums or not. You and I can both connect with the spirit world because we have a common denominator with those in spirit. They have a spirit body, and you have a spirit body within a physical body. This communication may result in spirit nudges for you, but through the same mechanism, it allows me to connect with the spirit world and translate their messages. Everyone has the ability to communicate through spirit bodies; it is your natural way of being and your birthright.

A WELL-ORCHESTRATED DESIGN

I am often asked about signs like yellow convertibles. Do our loved ones send signs? How does that work? Why am I not seeing them? Communication through signs, like any other kind of relationship, requires two people – two people searching for the best way to communicate.

The biggest misconception I encounter is that your communication with someone becomes one-sided after they pass. People mistakenly believe that without the help of a medium, they are powerless to reach out to someone after they pass. There is a belief that you simply have to wait to receive communication from the spirit world.

I know you have the ability to reach out and ask for communication.

I would like you to consider the ways you currently connect with the people you love most in the physical world. Do you send a text, write a letter, pick up the phone or meet for coffee? I believe that each one of these activities has an energetic equivalent. Sending a thought is like sending a text; they will get the message. Writing a message to them in your journal is like sending a letter; they will read it. Speaking out loud to them is like speaking over the phone; they will hear you. Setting aside a time to meet in meditation or inviting them along to a family gathering is like meeting them in person; they will be there. You can also ask for a specific sign.

Ask for a specific song, animal or word to come across your path. Be patient, because there is an orchestration in progress and it requires your willingness to listen and pay attention. The spirit world doesn't manifest yellow convertibles or butterflies out of thin air. A spirit nudge looks like glancing at the clock to see the same time over and over, seeing that same number in street signs, and then continuing to look at just the right time to spot it in licence plates.

A sign can be anything. One of my favourite signs was in a reading for Olivia. Her father showed me that he would send Olivia signs in the form of a little bunny rabbit. Her face lit up, and she told me that as a little girl she used to play a game with her father involving a small stuffed bunny rabbit. One of them would hide the bunny for the other – tucking it into a cupboard, hiding it under the sheets, or placing it under a T-shirt in a drawer. When the bunny was found, the finder would hide it so it could be found once again. Many years later in the spirit world, Olivia's father was still 'hiding' bunny rabbits for her to find. But he wasn't conjuring bunnies up out of thin air; he accomplished this by directing her to look or go in the direction of a bunny when it was nearby.

The scope of orchestrating a sign can be truly amazing. If you're a willing participant, I believe the spirit world can use you as a part of a larger picture. I think it's entirely possible that you've played a role in delivering a sign without even knowing it. Maybe you accidentally dropped a coin that was later found by a person whose father had collected them.

THE POWER OF SIGNS

I've personally experienced being a pawn in this larger design, and to this day it remains one of the most moving experiences I've ever been a part of. It started with my client, Amber. Amber came into my life when I was doing a show in Santa Monica. She had seen a poster of mine outside a small theatre there and felt pulled to enquire. The show was starting in one hour, and she was told that tickets were sold out, but if she waited and there was a no-show, she was welcome to come in. Luckily, there was a seat open, and she found a spot right at the very front. Amber's son had just passed from an overdose, and he was one of the first to come through that night.

Unbeknownst to me, sitting behind her during that show was my student, Shelly, and her son. Shelly's son was in his early twenties and was struggling with drug addiction; he was the same age and had the same addictions as Amber's son. I don't believe the two of them spoke that night, so they both went home with no idea that they had such similar stories.

On a random Tuesday morning two years later, I walked into a shop, and a woman who I vaguely recognised called out to me. 'Fleur! How are you?'

It was Amber. She reminded me she had been to a show of mine a few years ago and that she'd lost a son. She told me she had been to see her doctor at the hospital, and as she walked out of his office door, she'd spotted a feather on the ground. When she later told her doctor about finding it, he told her he found the likelihood of finding a giant black feather right outside his fifth-floor office door odd.

'I wasn't that surprised!' Amber continued. 'That's how my son communicates with me. I knew when I picked it up that this feather wasn't meant for me, and now I know it's meant for you!' she said as she handed the feather to me.

I thanked her, telling her I was touched. I carefully placed the feather in my bag and went about my shopping. Shortly thereafter, while loading my things into the car, I received a phone call telling me that my student, Shelly, had lost her son due to an overdose the previous night. Still in the car park, I called her immediately to pay my condolences.

We talked for a while. I told her I was sorry, and she reminded me that I had briefly met him once. Shelly and her son had attended a show of mine together, where they sat right behind a woman who had also lost her son to an overdose. She told me, 'My son and I were battling his addiction at that time, and it provided an incredibly healing moment to speak about it afterward. I often think back on that reading.'

My jaw dropped. I had just seen the same woman Shelly had sat behind in that show. In fact, I had Amber's feather – very obviously meant for Shelly – in my bag.

'Shelly, I have a feather for you.'

'How amazing!' she responded. 'A bird flew into my store this morning, and we had a hard time getting it out. I was sure it was Josh saying he'd made it safely.'

It is amazing that Amber's son knew to meet with Shelly's son in the spirit world to get a message to both ladies. It's hard to imagine how they placed all the puzzle pieces so perfectly in order for it to happen. I do know that everyone involved was paying attention, open to the intuitive nudges required to play this out. Amber knew to pick up the feather. She felt called to go to that shop, and I did as well. My friend intuitively knew it was important for me to call Shelly, and Shelly paid attention to the bird. When we're paying attention and we follow our inner nudges, incredible things can happen.

ELECTRICITY

I'm a rational psychic medium. If a lightbulb flickers or goes out, I'm the first to ask if it's screwed in all the way or propose that the filament in the bulb broke because it was old. From a philosophical perspective, I'm a strong proponent of the idea that if there are two explanations for an event, the simpler one is usually the true one.

Often this means a flashing light, which we think is spirit activity, is just a broken lightbulb filament. A light going out is more easily explained by an old lightbulb than by a spirit with a sense of humour. But I don't think that means the second is impossible. Just because I don't believe all flashing lights to be spirit activity doesn't mean I don't believe that some are.

I was doing a Q&A after a show of giving messages to an audience when the lights went out and turned back on. This wouldn't have been particularly remarkable, except that the only time it happened that night was immediately after someone stood up and asked, 'Can spirits affect electricity?' What more could I say than, 'Apparently so!'

Another humorous instance that made me contemplate a spirit's ability to affect electricity was during a phone reading for a woman in North Carolina. Ellen wanted to connect to her late boyfriend, a man she had dated for many years. I began the reading and felt a strong signal from David, who had been Ellen's romantic partner. David had led a dynamic life, and he'd been married twice. As we continued, David made reference to the fact that towards the end of his life, Ellen had nursed him and taken care of him, and he was very grateful.

At that point, I hesitated before noting that David still stayed in contact with his second wife. Ellen knew. 'He just couldn't say no,' she sighed.

I knew he had never asked Ellen to marry him, something she had wanted very much. In that moment, in my mind's eye I saw David down on one knee on the spirit side.

'He loves you, Ellen,' I said. 'He's sorry that he never asked you to marry him, he knew you wanted that.'

Ellen sighed with relief. 'I did wonder if he had really loved me,' she said. 'It's nice to know he did.'

In every reading, I leave some time for questions. Although you don't need a medium to ask questions for you (the spirit world can hear you easily), it can be nice to get an immediate answer. I asked Ellen if she had any questions and she did:

'When he would go MIA on those weekends in his truck, was he by himself?'

I paused. I wanted to get this right for Ellen. I returned my attention to David's spirit body. I felt a feeling of deep resistance to this question on David's side, and admittedly on mine, too.

I saw an image of David gambling on a trip, but he was not alone. 'Well,' I started tentatively, 'I see some gambling on those trips.' Ellen confirmed she knew about the gambling but quickly pressed on. 'I need a straight answer, was he alone. Yes or no.'

I decided to ignore David's resistance. She should know the truth; I would want to know. In that moment, just as I wanted to say, 'No, he wasn't alone,' Ellen's phone line went dead. When I say it went dead, I mean it really went dead. At the same time, I could tell David was *not* pleased with me.

'Sorry to piss you off,' I mumbled under my breath, joking a bit, 'but she really wanted to know!'

I tried to call her for five minutes, and it wouldn't connect. There was only a continuous busy tone. I even wrote her an email, saying, 'Ellen, I'm so sorry. I'm trying to call you back, but I can't seem to reach you. I'll keep trying.'

Finally, I was able to get her back on the phone. 'It was so strange,' she said. 'Both of my landline phones went dead. Nothing worked. In the time we were disconnected, I decided I don't think he wants me to know. He knew how insecure I was about his ex-wife. I guess he already told me he loves me, and that's all that matters now. I don't really need to know the answer to that question.'

Although I hesitate to say all electricity flukes are spirit activity, I think the potential for spirits to affect electricity is entirely possible – and hard to ignore at times.

UNEXPLAINABLE MAGIC

There's some magic to all of this. I have heard so many stories that I can't explain. Do you remember Beatrice from Chapter 9, whose husband Albert passed of suicide? Shortly after her reading she wrote me an email: 'In my reading you told me to watch for sunflowers as a sign, and I didn't think that made any sense; I never see sunflowers.'

'Shortly after my reading with you, seven sunflowers popped up in my yard. Those seven sunflowers thrived without any water for a long time but finally died. The next year, still in a dirt yard without any water, thirty sunflowers appeared, and what is so crazy is that they were a totally different variety from the first seven. I have lived in this house for twenty-nine years and never once was there ever a sunflower.'

She attached a photo of the sunflowers, and I really can't explain it. All I can say is it's simply *magic*.

At times, signs will make you feel a little crazy. 'Is it real?' 'Is it a coincidence?' 'Am I making it up?' are very common questions, and why wouldn't they be? Yet I challenge you to suspend disbelief, if even for a moment, because often signs are not a one-sided experience. It is easier for the spirit world to get your attention if you're open to recognising their communication.

Perhaps someone in the spirit world has been sending you ten million signs, and they've all been ignored or dismissed. It can be an enlightening exercise to imagine you are the spirit body trying to get someone's attention here in the physical world. How would you do it? What would you send?

Let's say you've been sending ladybirds for ten years. What a celebration there would be when finally one of your loved ones here in the physical world acknowledges the sign and says something like, 'Hey Dad, not sure if that's you, but I noticed the ladybirds!' If I were that person's father in the spirit world, I'd start sending a lot more ladybirds. In fact, that's exactly what happened to one of my clients. She told me that after acknowledging that exact sign, a few days later her car was covered in ladybirds. 'I don't need that many, Dad!' she told him, as she laughed.

I invite you to be your own medium and start a new relationship with your loved ones using signs, feelings and experiences as a new form of communication. Ask for a sign you want, and point out the ones you see. It's the start of a whole new form of communication, and I know your loved ones will respond.

DO IT YOURSELF

Take a moment to reflect on any and every sign you believe you have received from a loved one in the spirit world. Whether they be big signs or little ones, write them all down. Paying attention to signs is beneficial for both you and your loved ones in spirit. You benefit by taking inventory and slowing down enough to see the signs. Your loved ones on the other side benefit by knowing their signs are received.

Answer the following:

1. What do you believe are signs from your loved ones?
2. How have you seen them in the past?
3. What sign do you want to ask for right now?

Then, enter a passive meditation, and when you've found a point of stillness simply ask that the sign be offered to you in the next month.

CHAPTER 11

The Laws of the Spirit World

Jack, a spunky eight-year-old, gives a small sigh of exasperation as his mum leans forward to ask me, 'So where exactly *is* the spirit world?'

Jack rolls his eyes and says, 'Mom, right here, duh, we've been talking to them.'

The three of us have just finished a mediumship reading in which we connected to Jack's deceased older brother, Joey, who sadly passed away from a stroke at the young age of fourteen. Jack's eyes are wide as he takes it all in. His mum, who is sitting beside him on my couch, wipes away a tear.

Although it seems like a simple answer, I agree with Jack's assessment; the spirit world is right here. After ten years of psychic mediumship readings I have come to the very same conclusion that Jack, at eight, seems to think is so obvious. He has boiled down a seemingly hard question of 'Where is the spirit world?' with the easiest answer: *here*.

As they leave my office, Jack remembers that he has one last question: can I tell his brother to help him beat the next level of the video game he's playing? 'Totally,' I tell him as we're walking down the hall, 'in fact, you just told him yourself.'

I'm not saying that just to please this young boy. I do believe his older brother, Joey, is right there with us. In every reading I have done, without exception, the spirit world has indicated to me that while we may have a hard time entering their space, they enter ours without any problem.

As children, we find it easier to accept that there is a spirit world. Children hold a natural faith, while the adult brain is not as eager to accept these seemingly simple truths. We want rules so we can construct the spirit world in rational thought. I am no exception. In each reading I have given, I have weighed, measured, and asked questions in order to understand. While I know Jack is right when he says the spirit world is right here, I like rules. In my questions and interactions with members of the spirit world, I have found that the spirit world has a number of laws that hold steady across every reading.

- Law #1 – It is easy for the spirit world to enter our physical world and they do so without physical limitation. *They enter our world because they remain connected with us through purpose, love and joy.*
- Law #2 – Spiritual progress continues in the spirit world. *They learn and grow for spiritual expansion.*
- *Law* #3 – In the spirit world, passions and purpose continue. *They continue to interact with the passions they held while in the physical world, as well as passions they wished to pursue but couldn't.*
- Law #4 – The spirit world is aware of our lives in real time.

They continue to be aware of the big and small moments of our lives in real time.

- Law #5 – The spirit world exists in community. *They are connected to the people they knew in life, but also to strangers in order to be of service and offer strength whenever and wherever it is needed.*

In my more than 15,000 readings, every single spirit person has followed these five laws. Understanding that the spirit world operates in this capacity has given me a feeling of steadiness, a foundation upon which to place my understanding. It has made the spirit world more tangible, a structure I desperately craved as a young medium trying to understand what I was connecting to.

It's hard to find a place when you don't know what it looks like or how it works. Kids are much more capable of embracing the unknown than their adult counterparts; Jack finds these truths simple and straightforward. But the rest of us need a map. These laws of the spirit world give a foundation so that adults can make sense of it as well. I know that it is possible to have all people touch and experience the spirit world once they know where it is and how it works.

LAW #1: IT IS EASY FOR THE SPIRIT WORLD TO ENTER OUR PHYSICAL WORLD AND THEY DO SO WITHOUT PHYSICAL LIMITATION

I cannot imagine a better metaphor for relating you to the spirit world than the following: Two young fish are swimming along one day. Along comes an older, wiser fish. 'Good morning boys, he says. 'How's the water today?' The two younger fish continue swimming, floating along in silence. A few minutes later, one of the fish turns to the other and asks, 'What's water?'

You are the fish and the spirit world is the water. It's easy for us to swim around our whole lives never realising we are right in the middle of the spirit world. They are around you and beside you.

In my readings, the members of the spirit world all indicate that they are easily able to travel into our world. In fact, there is a constant back-and-forth of activity and communication happening between the two 'worlds'. Not only can they do it easily, but they do because our world continues to be a part of their reality. Life in the physical plane doesn't stop when the physical body leaves. It continues. Those in spirit show me that their purpose is directly linked to us, to the life they lived, or the experiences they shared with a community.

People often ask me in a panic after a reading, will my loved one reincarnate? Will they be gone for ever? I have never encountered this. While I do not know what does or doesn't happen with reincarnation, I do know that I have never had a reading in which I had to tell someone their person is no longer available. Nor will you ever cross to the spirit world yourself and be told you just missed them. As long as you live here, their purpose in connection to you continues. If they are a mother to you now, they will continue to be a mother in spirit. Purpose continues in many ways.

Linda was an older woman in her sixties who came to see me for a spirit communication reading in order to connect with her father. Yet when I turned my attention to the spirit world, I didn't immediately see her father. Instead, there were so many spirit people in the room I couldn't keep them all straight. In my mind's eye, they filled my office and streamed out of the door. One by one, they expressed their gratitude. As I connected, I found it strange that they had all suffered burns as part of their passing. When I expressed this to her, Linda told me she had worked as an ICU nurse in a burns unit for decades. It was clear that the many people assembled in my tiny office were here to say thank you to Linda for her love and care.

Next in line was her father, whose purpose in being connected with her was different but equally strong. He had not been present in her life when she was a younger woman, and he conveyed that he was doing his best to be a better father to her now.

All relationships are eternal and all spirit people will and can connect with you. Whether someone was or wasn't a good parent, spouse or friend, their relationship with you is purpose-driven and it never ends.

A point of concern I often hear from my clients is that they think if they speak to their loved ones in spirit, then they will not be at peace. I promise you aren't waking anyone up or disturbing their rest; they are peacefully awake and eager to engage. Whether you speak to them or not, the spirit world is never stagnant and stationary. It does not require energy or effort for them to be in connection with you; it is effortless.

Not only can the spirit world enter our world with ease, but it has also become very clear to me that the limitations we experience do not hold true in the spirit world. Physical space is no obstacle for those who are passed. In readings, many spirit people speak about visiting their home country again, travelling alongside us here in the physical world, and seeing parts of the world they had always wanted to see but never had the opportunity to in their physical life.

I recall a reading in which I connected to a man who was incredibly proud of his American citizenship. I knew that he had made it to the United States by fleeing his country. He showed me that his home country was dangerous and that for that reason, his daughter had never been able to visit it. He repeated over and over again that although he had been able to return there from the spirit world, he did not want his daughter to go. She should stay in this new country. His daughter nodded and told me that he was born in North Korea, a country that continues to be very dangerous for travellers, and that she certainly had no plans to travel there at this time.

It is also not uncommon for those in spirit to travel alongside those in the physical world. Many spirit people have been able to communicate correctly the various places their ashes were spread or the vacations their family and friends have taken. When there is no physical body, there are no physical limitations.

LAW #2 – SPIRITUAL PROGRESS CONTINUES IN THE SPIRIT WORLD

Ashley was thirty-two but she sounded like a lost, small girl. When she introduced herself, her voice shook slightly with nerves. Right away, I knew she had suffered great losses and my heart hurt for her as I said, 'You've lost a baby that you wanted to have very much.' Upon hearing this, Ashley began to cry.

I felt a grandmother step in as if to comfort her, and I said, 'Your grandmother shows me that you have been struggling with extreme depression and have returned home to live with your parents.' I continued, 'She needs you to know that you don't need to feel guilty and you need to forgive yourself.' Her grandmother was not the only one present and next, I felt a younger man in spirit step forward on my right. My first understanding of this young man was that he had passed suddenly of an overdose. I sensed a romantic connection to Ashley, but I did not feel that there had been a commitment between the two of them.

Ashley hesitated but confirmed that she had known someone like that.

I had the strong urge to tell Ashley that her former partner begged her to never again date someone like him. He made me feel that his actions had not been kind. 'He is insistent that you raise the bar when you begin to date again.' I told her. I heard the name 'Michael', and she confirmed the name.

Michael went on to recognise that his actions had placed an incredible mental strain on her, that he had pushed her to give up the baby they had created, and that he had not shown her love. He saw that his actions had caused her to go into a deep depression. Michael was insistent that Ashley increase her self-worth and that she not allow another person like him to enter her life. He emphasised that this was an experience of growth for both of them.

Michael taught me that those in the spirit world are able to self-reflect and thereby grow. He had indicated spiritual growth and a continuation of the ability to see the consequences of his actions from the other side.

No one on the other side is unchanging and stuck. I have seen the transition to spirit encourage tremendous growth in people. This growth is so integral to the spirit world that it shows up in almost every reading I do. Those in the spirit world relay messages around changes in beliefs, apologies and messages of love – earlier unexpressed – to those left behind.

LAW #3 – IN THE SPIRIT WORLD, PASSIONS AND PURPOSE CONTINUE

You take your passions with you. Those in spirit want to be here because they love you but their participation can also hold a purpose beyond their connection to those they leave behind. I first learned about the spirit world's involvement in our world in a reading I did for Elyse, who asked me afterwards, 'Can you ask my father what he is doing? Does he have a purpose?'

I took a moment, trying to translate it correctly. 'Well if I'm seeing this right,' I started, 'it's a little strange. He speaks of being an inventor for the world, just like while he was here.'

'That's correct,' she said, 'he was an inventor here and was always taking things apart and making them work better.'

I continued a little more confidently. I certainly had never said anything like this before. 'The best way I can describe it is that your father is inventing things on an energetic level, preparing them for inventors. It's almost like I see him creating ideas, with the hope that someone will grab them out of thin air, here, out of the ether into this world.'

'I think that sounds just like him,' she said.

Elyse's dad is creating inventions in the ether in the hope that someone here in our world will be open to their undirected intuition and will identify that idea and give it life.

Certainly, we have heard this concept reflected in our own world. Musicians, artists, even scientists have spoken about muses, about ideas that seemed to be delivered from outside of the artist.

Lauren's grandfather worked in a similar way on the other side. I started the reading by saying, 'Your father's father has passed, you see that? He comes to you on the left.' Lauren answered that he had. She and her mother grabbed each other's hands. This was the person they wanted to connect with.

Immediately, Lauren's grandfather brought my attention to teaching and I said to Lauren, 'Somebody works with kids on a regular basis. Is that you?' She responded that she was in fact a teacher. I continued, 'He talks about working with kids and he's very proud of that work. He must have been a teacher too, and I feel it is a profession that he actually has a very, very high regard for. I think he would've told you that.'

In a later email, she wrote to me that her grandfather, Joseph, had taught almost every age and level during his expansive educational career. He had spent a total of forty-one years working as an educator, but arguably his favourite years were those he spent at San Jose State University teaching adults in the credential and administrative credential programmes.

Her grandfather had more to say during the reading. I continued, 'I think he feels like he's got some expertise on it and a sense of, "I can give you some pointers." Where he's saying, "I'm gonna be watching over your shoulder." I think he continues teaching on the other side. It feels so important to him.'

Lauren and her mother continued to wipe away tears as we finished the reading and I was left with a deep awe for this educator who was continuing his dedication on the other side. It is little surprise that a man with such love for his work would continue to be intimately involved from the spirit world. I know that he is not only aware of what Lauren is doing in her classroom but also continues to intuitively guide her and other educators – a job he's happy to do.

Based on this experience, it may seem that all members of the spirit world continue the job they had here. That's not the case. Some spirit people speak of simply relaxing and they make it very clear they want nothing to do with the job they left behind. Passions and purpose take many forms. I've had fisherman say they spend their time watching and revitalising our oceans, or mothers say they're keeping an eye on their kids and grandkids. Often purpose in relationships continues – a mother continues to be a mother, a grandfather continues the relationship of being a grandfather, and a child continues to stay in connection with their parents and siblings. I also believe there are activities those in the spirit world are engaged with that I have no point of reference for and thereby no way to communicate.

Regardless of their role in our lives or work, each person on the other side has a continuation of life, passions and personal growth.

LAW #4: THE SPIRIT WORLD IS AWARE OF OUR LIVES IN REAL TIME

'Your dad tells me you still can't whistle,' I said to Ben, my twelve-year-old client. Ben sheepishly grinned at me and looked at his mum, who gave him a wink. I told him that his dad has seen him practising the whistle in his bedroom, right beside a pillowcase made out of his dad's old shirts. 'Keep practising,' his dad said, 'you'll get it one day.' Ben didn't say a word but his mum reached over to give him a squeeze and told me she used to whistle with Brent, Ben's dad, while they teased their son for not being able to, and yes, they turned a few shirts into a pillowcase.

Ben beamed when I told him his dad was proud that he was learning to play not just one instrument but two, and laughed when I told him that when it comes to his bossy grandma, he's allowed to ignore her. She was always telling his dad what to do, too. 'She is pretty bossy,' he responded.

I am often amazed by these small moments the spirit world sees. It encourages the question of how we make time in our life to spend with those on the other side.

I promise the spirit world isn't watching your every move – they don't care about your bathroom habits. But they do care about the important moments in your life, small or large. This is not so different from the way we interact with our friends and family in our own daily life. While we check in regularly with each other to see how things are going, no two separate people are involved in each other's lives each moment of the day. In the spirit world, their relationship to you holds the same dynamic. When you have exciting news to share, they are aware of that.

For celebrations, they join you. In moments of sadness, you come together to grieve. Sometimes, they just like to join you for a cup of coffee. They are aware of your days and engaged with you and your life as it is happening.

The spirit world has often shown me that the spirits of our loved ones are aware of our joy as much as our pain. They keep us company in the times that are hard.

The overarching truth remains simple: the spirit world is right *here*.

LAW #5 – THE SPIRIT WORLD EXISTS IN COMMUNITY AND IS AVAILABLE TO YOU WHENEVER YOU NEED THEM

Sienna was late for our appointment, and when her face appeared on my phone screen I could see why. She had a fussy, sick baby on her hip and she herself looked like she had just rolled out of bed. The second I started the reading, I was hit by a tremendous amount of depression in her spirit body.

It was overwhelming and I wanted a 'second opinion'; I shifted to the spirit world to find Sienna's kind, strong grandmother. After a few identifying features, Sienna's grandmother brought my awareness to Sienna's past, particularly the abusive experiences she had endured. I asked Sienna, 'Do you understand that you have been emotionally and physically abused in the past?' Sienna answered that she had, and that she was preparing to speak at a trial later that week to face a massage therapist who had sexually abused many women including herself. To make matters even more horrifying, Sienna had been recommended this massage therapist in her recovery work from an abusive partner.

Sienna's grandmother showed me thirty-five counts of sexual abuse. 'Yes', Sienna said, 'there were thirty-five women at the start of the trial but there are only four of us left. The others were dismissed. I have to speak as one of the four.' All of a sudden, I felt many many spirit people enter the room. They filled the whole space. I turned back to Sienna to tell her, 'When you speak this week in court, not only will you have the power of those thirty-five women, but those in spirit stand beside you. Anyone in the spirit world who has ever loved one of those thirty-five women will join you when you speak. They will offer their power and their love. They are asking that you know you are never alone. Close your eyes before you enter the courtroom and ask for strength. Feel their arms around you. They will be there.'

This reading touched me greatly. Those in spirit want to be of service. They love fiercely and their purpose continues in the spirit world, often intertwining with our own. It is always okay to ask for strength. In times of need, they will always be there.

Sienna texted me the week after our reading to tell me that our session had given her so much strength and courage going into the court proceedings. She was relieved to tell me that on the day of what would have been her grandparents' seventieth wedding anniversary, her aggressor was sentenced to five years for rape and sexual assaults. I believe the anniversary date is significant, a nod from her grandmother that she was present to offer the strength Sienna had asked for.

A human life is a life of shared experiences. We are connected to everyone who has ever gone through a similar experience or a similar trial, and that does not end when we cross. Those in spirit congregate around people they know, but also those in need whom they have never met.

If you ever hit a time of difficulty in your life, extend a prayer to be lifted up. There are no strangers in the spirit world. Love and strength are always freely given.

DO IT YOURSELF

1. Find twenty minutes today to do a walking meditation with your favourite music. Pick a space in which you can truly let go and walk without worrying about traffic or other distractions. As you walk, invite your loved ones in spirit along. Ask them to hold your hands and walk with you.

2. Call upon a person in the spirit world for help today to give you strength and clarity about an event in your life that is currently causing you grief or trouble. You can write a letter or ask in a meditation.

Journal prompt:
Write about what you believe happens when we cross over.

CHAPTER 12

Faith

On a flight coming back from London, Ray, one of the flight attendants on board, stopped me by the bathrooms and asked me what I did for work. It was such a direct question that it took me by surprise. Many times when asked this question, I avoid the truth and answer with 'grief therapist' or 'life coach'. Yet there was something about Ray and his directness that made me say, 'I'm a medium, I talk to people who have passed.'

'Oh wow,' he said, with the slightest hint of a Texas accent. 'I'm not sure about that, but I am a believer,' pointing to the leather Bible with glistening gold-lined pages placed right next to the drinks cart.

He poked his head around the corner to quickly check on his other passengers. Satisfied, he continued, 'As a believer, I know one thing to be true, and that's that I don't know it all.' There was a long pause. 'Do you want some coffee? I'll tell you a story.'

He busied himself with the coffee pot, handed me a styrofoam cup and, while leaning on his cart, jumped back into his tale.

'When my daughter was about five, she's about your age now,

we owned a gas station. She'd help me put up the numbers each morning with a long pole and suction cups. This was back in the day when gas was ninety-nine cents to the gallon, but because we owned the gas station we filled up our own car there and never paid for gas.

'One day I took my daughter on a road trip far away from home. We needed gas so while I stood at the station, I told her to go in and get herself a candy bar while I filled up the tank. "Mom wouldn't like it," she protested. I threw my hands up. I told her, "It's vacation! Get yourself that candy bar, girl."

'My littlest walked herself into the gas station, selected her KitKat bar and presented it at the cashier. She was so little, the cashier had to peer over the counter to tell my girl that it would be sixteen dollars, please. When she came out the door her face looked very worried as she told me, "Mommy really won't be happy. Not only are we eating chocolate, but we spent a lot of money on it! Sixteen dollars!"

'I had to explain to her the candy only cost a few cents, but we also had to pay for gas. Until this moment, she hadn't understood that gas costs money. I explained that at the gas station we owned, people paid us too. I'll never forget her reaction. She looked up at me and said, "Daddy, what else don't I know?"

'That question has stayed with me.' He pointed a finger back at his Bible on the drink cart. 'When someone tells me something I want to immediately discount, I look up at the big man in the sky and ask, "What else don't I know?"'

I left the plane thinking about Ray and I've carried his question with me. It's a very open-minded question, requiring the asker to consider that you'll never know it all.

I have always strongly admired those who have a steadfast faith in something larger than themselves. I found that kind of belief to be incredibly hard to come by as a teenager and in my early twenties. I wanted to be like Ray the flight attendant, a person who seemed to hold a natural trust. But I couldn't find it at that time. In my early years I felt like I was always, in all ways, questioning.

These early doubts may be one of the reasons I initially became a good medium; I wanted the evidence and I looked for it incessantly. I wanted proof. This shifted. Now I hold a knowing and the faith I was looking for.

It was a woman from Cambodia who changed the trajectory of my readings and helped me make room for faith. When she came in for a medium reading, I started it like any other. I described her father and dove head first into the 'evidence'. I told her every fact I could receive from him, the more specific the better, down to the shoes he liked to wear.

About twenty minutes into the reading, she leaned forward and gently put her hand on my knee. 'I know he's here, you don't have to prove it. What does he have to say?' I was absolutely floored. From my own western perspective, there was never enough evidence. I felt like I needed to get as detailed as possible because, in my mind, I could never offer enough.

I understand her better now. In my ten years of working as a medium, I still like evidence but I no longer see it as the destination. Don't get me wrong, I love the proof in mediumship, the stuff that comes out that makes the entire audience go *how did she know that?* I love it because it offers a bridge for people like me, who have a hard time believing stuff without tangible evidence.

Yet, I have also come to know that faith is an important part of the equation. If you want absolute proof that an afterlife exists, there will never be enough evidence in the world to give you that. At some point, we have to have our own faith and form our own beliefs. This is an internal process and no amount of external proof will get you there.

While my own life experiences have left me with little doubt that life continues in some way, it would be silly to say there is absolutely no doubt. There are days where I wake up in the morning and I think to myself, *do I really talk to dead people? This is crazy.* But then I start my readings and I am once again reminded of the astounding information and healing available. Most of all, I *feel* the spirit world right there. While this isn't evidential science in the least bit, it makes it a very real experience for me. I know that through the techniques you have completed throughout this book, and with a little bit of faith in yourself along with a faith in something larger than yourself, you can feel this connection as well.

WORKING ALONGSIDE TRADITIONAL THERAPY

When I first started doing readings in 2008, psychic medium work was still largely unknown. Most people had no idea what I was talking about when I told them I worked as a medium. Now, it is rare that someone misunderstands and thinks I am talking about my clothing size.

A few years ago, I began to see a massive shift in the way psychic mediums were treated in the media and among mental health professionals. It is not unusual for my clients to tell me that they were referred to me by therapists, psychiatrists, and even medical doctors. At first I thought this was a fluke. I envisioned one very open-minded, nutty doctor recommending patients to a psychic medium. Amazingly, this has not been the case, and many doctors have recommended me over the years. I have read for entire grief groups and for grief organisations. I can't express how happy this makes my heart, because I know the good it can do. There is an open-mindedness emerging in the world that I find exciting. Healing takes a village and I appreciate that others are starting to see that readings can play a significant role in the healing process.

What is most exciting is that we are no longer stuck on the question *is it real?* There are bigger, more interesting questions to ask, not only *how does it work?* but also, *how can it heal?*

I have personally witnessed this work to be a catalyst in grief. It certainly doesn't replace grief therapy in any way, but it can be a modality that offers new and different breakthroughs for people. I see myself as part of a community that aims to offer people new ways to move forward and for that reason I too often refer people back to grief therapists.

One of the first grief therapists I worked with, Claire Bidwell Smith, vocalises this beautifully in our podcast *Moving Beyond*. In the introduction she explains her current view on mediums, from her standpoint as a grief therapist. She says,

'. . . after a while I stopped caring if it was real, and I decided what was more important was how it made people feel. A good session with a psychic medium can turn things around for someone who is lost in their grief. I've seen it time and time again. I could have a client who was completely stuck, despite doing all the right things: allowing themselves to grieve, working through their emotions, reviewing their relationships with the person they lost, going to grief groups, making amends, you name it. But still they would be stuck with *something* that happened with the death or some unresolved aspect of their relationship. After a good mediumship reading, they would come away with a completely new understanding. They would come away with a feeling of connection to their loved one and often a bit of closure.'

I am grateful for practitioners like Claire, as their open-mindedness can help people find the healing they need. In my ten years of working as a medium, I am convinced that healing, expansion and growth are the reasons I do readings. It brings me joy to see that others are starting to see the impact they can have as well.

HEALING

I know the healing that a psychic mediumship reading offers is real. Like Claire, I've seen it countless times. I see it energetically and I see it physically manifested in the weight that lifts off people's shoulders, the tears of relief, and even the laughs we share in my office. This work is not about whether there is an afterlife, or whether I am right or wrong; it is about how people are able to take the next step in processing their grief.

Whenever I am scared or nervous to do a big show, old beliefs creep up for me, always on the same rotation. 'What if they think I'm crazy?' 'What if it doesn't work?' 'What if I look foolish?'

What stops these thoughts dead in their tracks is, *this is not about me.*

That is the truth. It has never been about me. My job is to get out of the way so that healing can take place. I've been lucky to witness tremendous healing through mediumship, and to remind me, I have a wall in my office covered with thank-you notes. They remind me of the healing possibilities that can lie on the other side of a good reading. I look at them when I need to be reminded of the magic.

Some of these notes are sweet and simple: 'I was nervous, but it left me with this strange knowing my mom was really ok.' Or, 'This is what I needed to move forward. I left speechlessly light.'

Others seem to shift people's trajectories in a stronger way:

'I can sleep again', 'I feel like I have my wife back, she's no longer hiding from the world in grief' and 'This honestly healed my soul.'

One reading that greatly touched my heart was for my parents' beloved neighbour, Phoebe. She lived alone, had lost all her family members, and was battling cancer with only her dog, Mister, by her side. After our reading together, she wrote to tell me she was no longer afraid of dying. I had not considered this kind of healing before. Phoebe passed shortly thereafter.

I no longer read from a place of having to know it all or get all the details. Healing is the destination. Feeling connection to each other and to our passed loved ones is my intention. Peace is my ultimate goal. While the details in a reading are important, there will always be some mystery in how it all works.

A good reading can reunite someone with their own spirit and remind them that they are more than a physical body. This can bring peace to the mind and body. At the end of the day my hope is that people leave a session and implement the feeling of connection into their lives.

I end my sessions by telling my client that they can do this kind of connecting all on their own. I am not the access point to their loved ones. Their loved ones exist around them and are connected to them even when I am not in the room. I am simply operating as a literal medium, the bridge, to show that it is possible to bridge two worlds and offer communication. Your connection to your loved ones is stronger than anything I can have in our time together. You don't need me to connect; you know their signal, so you can reach them at any time. Faith is required to fill the gap.

THE ORIGIN OF SPIRITUAL CONNECTION

A dear friend of mine had the opportunity to meet Jane Goodall, 'the woman who lived with apes'. As a child I idolised her, so when over lunch he casually told me he was collecting questions to ask her, I almost launched out of my seat with excitement. 'I have one!' I exclaimed. I knew exactly what I wanted to ask: did Jane Goodall believe in an afterlife, and did she believe that the primates have an understanding of the afterlife or worship something outside of themselves?

A few days later I received a video from him. There I saw Jane Goodall, sitting on a bench with the Wyoming mountains at her back. In the video, my friend turns to her and asks if she believes in an afterlife. Realising that this is perhaps a sensitive subject, he quickly follows it by saying, 'I know that's a tough question.' Jane Goodall brilliantly replies, 'no it's not!'

In the little video clip I was sent, Jane told him that she does believe in the afterlife and had felt a great spiritual power in the forest. She also believed herself to have been in communication with people who had died while in the stillness of the forest.

Perhaps the most profound part of her answer was when she spoke about the chimpanzees and their worship. Jane said 'The chimpanzees do amazing ritual displays with this amazing waterfall that drops eighty feet. I believe that if they could actually speak, talk to each other, that they might very well turn this into some kind of mystic religion, worship of the sun, the stars, things that we don't understand.'

I was thrilled with Jane's answer because I believe that faith and a desired connection to all creation is more a natural way of life for us than an unnatural deviation. Jane Goodall has witnessed that we as humans are not the only beings who perceive something outside of ourselves as sacred. She observed that honouring divinity supersedes language.

Jane Goodall's experiences and answer to my question have made me wonder where our need for connection comes from. Perhaps worship and faith are not just human intelligence assets, but rather are internally and universally present. Could it be that the search for *something more* and connection to faith is a natural part of us? Perhaps the search for higher meaning is not the construct of an intelligent mind but originates in the deeper wisdom that inherently lives within all of us.

While we consider ourselves more intellectually focused than the primates of the world, I encourage you not to forget this natural part of you. To worship, to connect, to find meaning, are all primal needs. We do not 'learn' to feel spiritually connected; rather, we have to return to and honour our natural spiritual core, like the chimpanzees. It is our rational brain that wants the evidence, but when we allow ourselves to relax into feeling and experience, we don't really need all the details.

Anything that connects you to the feeling of awe aligns you with your spirit core. The experience of returning to faith is not meant to be difficult. I encourage you to find ways to experience the divine that feel right to you: through the arts, animals, people, walking in nature. It is truly that simple.

SPIRITUAL PRACTICE

When you know that we are part of, and never separated from, the spirit world, you change the way you walk through life. The moment you become conscious that your spirit exists and can connect to other spirits, even if for a fleeting second, is a very powerful moment. I see my work as one of these vehicles to the spirit core. A reading is meant to reunite the person I am reading for with the thing they have known all along: *you are so much more than your physical being*. When someone feels lost, a good reading can be the catalyst that returns them to this natural and eternal knowing. But this feeling will likely fade. Rather than seek out reading after reading, I encourage my clients to find the feeling of connection within themselves. Retaining the knowledge is part of a spiritual practice.

I don't think people need regular readings. We are all offered daily opportunities to be awestruck by life; the visceral moment in which you know there to be more than your physical self. You can feel this by looking out into an ocean stretching far out in front of you, by holding a newborn baby, listening to a particularly beautiful piece of music, or sitting in a chapel where people have worshipped for hundreds of years before you. When you stop long enough to appreciate your world it opens you up to your own divinity.

If you have encountered these awesome moments, you have also had the experience of losing them. Our twenty-first-century world is not built for spiritual communion, we have to actively create time and space for it. While we forget, we can also choose a practice to remember and search for the moments of wonder in daily life.

A spiritual practice is anything that regularly realigns you with your own divinity and that 'something larger'. It is called a spiritual practice because you have to practise it. It has to start within because your connection to anything outside of you cannot exist without you first establishing a connection to your internal self.

Many students work with me and desire to be better mediums. They are often disappointed when I start them off with the intuitive practices we covered in the first chapters. I do this because any spiritual gift you have starts within. To attain greater stability, focus and integrity in psychic or mediumship work, you have to work on the self first.

The exercises in this book can act as a spiritual practice. If, in reading this book, you find yourself frustrated by the practices or still unable to feel, see or hear in the ways you desire, I recommend that you begin by daily placing yourself in the way of beauty. A spiritual practice can be as simple as taking a walk outside to look at the amazing nature that exists around you in both big and small ways. It can be two minutes in which you close your eyes and breathe. None of this has to be complicated and none of it is right or wrong. There is no greater spiritual authority than your own inner voice and there is no greater spiritual place of worship than within.

THE SEEKER

You are a spirit body with a signal, and your signal holds a vibration that aligns with an interest in the awakening of your spiritual consciousness. I know this vibration exists within you because you would not have picked up this book, or it would not have been given to you, if that alignment didn't exist. If most of your blueprints and current were not in alignment with a desire to access your own spiritual truths, this book would not have found you in that moment. It would have been impossible.

This makes one of the key purposes in your life that of a 'seeker'. A seeker is an individual who is looking for their own truths and connection to something larger in this life. This can be a lifelong purpose or a purpose presented in this moment of your life, but if you have read this book it is a part of your spirit core. Everyone who finds themselves in my office or in one of my classes shares this commonality; they hold a deep desire, sometimes consciously unknown, that seeks to realign their conscious mind with their spirit within.

While this book may have ended, this isn't the end of your journey A seeker's journey is through experience, not lecture. With a little faith in yourself you will have these experiences yourself. One thing I know for sure: when you seek to move beyond, you will always find a way.

DO IT YOURSELF

1. Plan a moment this week to put yourself in the way of beauty. Go out in nature, watch a sunrise or sunset, or seek out a space you find particularly spiritual.
2. Write about a time when you felt most connected to your divinity.
3. Journal about the ways in which you are seeking for truth and meaning and what you have discovered so far. Have your beliefs shifted through your lifetime?

Epilogue

Consciousness, your life force, the soul – it is all still a mystery. Prior to my career as a medium, I searched for spirit in other places and I was sure I would work as a neuroscientist. My obsession started early, at sixteen when I first heard about neuroplasticity, the idea that the brain is adaptable. Prior to this discovery, it was widely believed that the brain was fixed in structure and function.

For my science fair project that year, I wanted to know if neuroplasticity applied to animals. I was particularly curious about toads; I had learned that they don't actually see their prey as prey, they eat as a reflex response to a visual change in light when a cricket (or anything) moves. In the project, I asked: if I kept my toads in the dark for a week, would I observe their brains' reflex centres to change to accommodate for other senses, just like a human's brain adapts when needed?

That year, I spent all of my midnights with six toads, newly acquired from the local pet shop. I hoped to show the world that their brains had changed due to a changed environment. It sounds crazy now, me and a bunch of toads up at all hours of the night, but that project sent me to the prestigious International Science and Engineering Fair that year and offered many opportunities to speak about my research.

(The toads lived a happy life in my bedroom after this experiment.)

At a state-wide symposium, I presented my research paper to a panel and then took questions. A man raised his hand and asked, while looking down at my thick research report, if I stood by my statement that I had 'proven' the toads' behaviour to change. Confused, I responded that yes, the p-values I calculated showed statistical significance to prove my null hypothesis. 'Wrong!' he bellowed. 'There is no such thing as proving something in the scientific world. There is only evidence. Why would you possibly believe you can prove anything?!' He was so angry about it. I responded with silence, and trembled. It was very clear to me that I had messed this science thing up completely.

Later, after the take-down, someone explained to the very shaken up sixteen-year-old me that 'proof' is a dirty word in science and no one should ever use it. We can't prove a theory to be correct because future evidence, yet to be discovered, could exist and could be inconsistent with that theory. Research can support or correlate, but it cannot prove.

I was pretty mortified then, but now I feel like the whole proof conundrum lets me, and all of us, off the hook. Am I sure there is a spirit world? That intuition is real? That psychic ability exists and you have it too? No, I can't prove it. I know that I never ever will be able to – I am afraid science won't let anyone do that. On the flip side, no one can prove that it doesn't exist. Herein lies the magic, space to explore the unknown, and the search for more. There is much left to uncover and I believe the key is to keep an open mind; once you close the door and dismiss something entirely you can't study it.

While I am convinced a spirit world exists, the sixteen-year-old researcher in me will always allow a little scepticism in my life for good scientific measure – and I will keep it that way. Scepticism doesn't have to get in the way of experience. I keep an open mind because I know that my world, and what lies beyond, is infinite in its potential – as long as I can stay curious. That is my dream for us all. Scepticism does not limit our potential, closed minds do.

Reading and Resources

BOOKS

The Highly Sensitive Person: How to Thrive When the World Overwhelms You, Elaine N. Aron

The Gifts of Imperfection, Brené Brown

The Awakened Mind: Biofeedback and the Development of Higher States of Awareness, C. Maxwell Cade

When Things Fall Apart: Heart Advice for Difficult Times, Pema Chödrön

The Body Keeps the Score: Mind, Brain and Body in the Transformation of Trauma, Bessel van der Kolk

Insight Meditation: A Step-by-step Course on How to Meditate, Sharon Salzberg and Joseph Goldstein

The Seat of the Soul, Gary Zukav

PRACTITIONERS

Liz Andolong
Reiki, mindfulness and intuitive coach
www.lizandolong.com

Alua Arthur
Death doula training and end-of-life planning
www.goingwithgrace.com

Kasey Crown
Integrative psychotherapist and trauma healing workshops
www.kaseycrown.com

Amy Fleetman
Acupuncturist, herbalist and medical intuitive
www.fleetmanacupuncture.com

Claire Bidwell Smith
Grief expert and author
www.clairebidwellsmith.com

Carly Taylor
Integrative embodiment coach
www.gingerpai.com

Acknowledgements

This book exists because thousands of people have given me the great privilege of connecting with them in readings, classes and on stage. If you crossed my path at any point, you helped shape this book and I thank you.

MOM: I would not have found the energy or courage to be a working psychic medium if it wasn't for you. You have done it all – you were my first assistant, my first editor, my number one cheerleader and most importantly my mom on the hard days. Thank you for never letting me forget who I am, even when I wanted to. All of me exists freely because you cleared the way.

DAD: You have helped me move any mountain I face, even flying back and forth on the same day to pick up Phoebe so I could focus on teaching and writing. In a world of 'no's you always remind me, 'Nee heb je, ja kun je krijgen.' All I know about integrity and hard work I learned from you; thank you for giving me my backbone so I could get the 'yes's.

LOTTE: The best luck of my life was getting you as a sister. You are there for the giggles and for the tears, for the reality checks and for the unconditional love. I don't know what I would do without you – you make me feel like as long as we have each other, we can do anything (. . . dare I say it, even bookkeeping).

BEN MAWSON: Thank you for believing in me from the start and for enthusiastically reading every version of this book imaginable. You have a magic power to build bridges so that others can share their many gifts with the world. I am insanely lucky to have your help in building mine.

MATILDA FORBES WATSON: The moment I met you, I thought 'she gets it', and you did. Thank you for your commitment to making this book come alive in the most authentic way possible and making it better than I ever thought it could be.

OLIVIA: You wear so many hats and you wear them so stylishly. Thank you for being my right-hand woman and for keeping my life afloat so that I could fully dive into writing this book.

LEMON LODGE CREW (HEATHER, DARWIN, JACKI, JOHN, JARED, KASEY, DANI(S), SAM, CARLY, ASHTON, JOSH, MAURICIO): When I showed up ten years ago looking for a place to live, I did not realise I would walk out with my chosen LA family. You were all the first people I allowed to see the full, authentic me because you were your authentic selves, too. In ways too many to count and too long to write out, you have supported in running my business, helping at shows,

ACKNOWLEDGEMENTS

watching Phoebe, hours of filming, editing and sound work. Most of all, you have supported my heart; thank you from the bottom of it.

AMY, DANI, DANIELLE, CARLY, CLAIRE, JAY, KRISTEN, LIZ, MATT, MIKEY, SAM, TRACI: Little snippets and stories of our lives made it into this book. Thank you for being a part of this ride and sharing this life with me. You all keep it fun, love-filled and a true adventure. Never in my wildest dreams could I have thought up better friendships.

TONY STOCKWELL: You have been my north star. Not just for your astounding mediumship work, but also for the humility with which you offer it. Thank you for lighting the way for so many.

DANIELLE: Who would have known, back when I was in the literal closet, that ten years later you would help edit my book. Thank you for reading so many drafts and helping the book find its legs.

KASEY CROWN: The knowledge of embodiment that you shared with me in the years when I wrote this book is now instrumental in how I teach. Thank you for being a true teacher to me.

CAROLYN THORNE: I am so lucky to bring this book out with you at the helm. It is such an honour to be in your hands. Thank you for seeing the value in this book from the start.

CANDACE JOHNSON: Thank you for helping me find my writer's voice, a process that felt so daunting at the start. You helped me identify what I wanted to write and how to write it.

About the Author

Fleur Leussink has been named one of the 'Best Mediums in Los Angeles' by CBS and *LA Magazine*. Her innate ability to directly communicate with loved ones 'in spirit' has connected countless families from all around the world. In Los Angeles she is largely sought after in the entertainment industry; doing readings for well known A-list musicians, actors and politicians.

Fleur first discovered her gift as a young girl. Starting at the age of four, spirits visited her bedroom at night and she saw auras around people. However, it was many years later, while attending UCLA as a pre-med student, that she gave her first reading. Word of mouth spread quickly, and after graduating, she began giving readings full time. Residing between Lisbon and Los Angeles with her dog Phoebe, Fleur is on a mission to connect as many people as she can to their loved ones on the other side.

books to help you live a good life

Join the conversation and tell
us how you live a #goodlife

🐦 @yellowkitebooks
📘 YellowKiteBooks
📌 Yellow Kite Books
📷 YellowKiteBooks